COMPREHENSIVE RESEARCH
AND STUDY GUIDE

Langston
Hughes

BLOOM'S

M A J O R

POETS

EDITED AND WITH AN INTRODUCTION
BY HAROLD BLOOM

BLOOM'S MAJOR DRAMATISTS

Anton Chekhov
Henrik Ibsen
Arthur Miller
Eugene O'Neill
Shakespeare's Comedies
Shakespeare's Histories
Shakespeare's Romances
Shakespeare's Tragedies
George Bernard Shaw
Tennessee Williams

BLOOM'S MAJOR NOVELISTS

Jane Austen
The Brontës
Willa Cather
Charles Dickens
William Faulkner
F. Scott Fitzgerald
Nathaniel Hawthorne
Ernest Hemingway
Toni Morrison
John Steinbeck
Mark Twain
Alice Walker

BLOOM'S MAJOR SHORT STORY WRITERS

William Faulkner
F. Scott Fitzgerald
Ernest Hemingway
O. Henry
James Joyce
Herman Melville
Flannery O'Connor
Edgar Allan Poe
J. D. Salinger
John Steinbeck
Mark Twain
Eudora Welty

BLOOM'S MAJOR WORLD POETS

Geoffrey Chaucer
Emily Dickinson
John Donne
T. S. Eliot
Robert Frost
Langston Hughes
John Milton
Edgar Allan Poe
Shakespeare's Poems & Sonnets
Alfred, Lord Tennyson
Walt Whitman
William Wordsworth

BLOOM'S NOTES

The Adventures of Huckleberry Finn
Aeneid
The Age of Innocence
Animal Farm
The Autobiography of Malcolm X
The Awakening
Beloved
Beowulf
Billy Budd, Benito Cereno, & Bartleby the Scrivener
Brave New World
The Catcher in the Rye
Crime and Punishment
The Crucible

Death of a Salesman
A Farewell to Arms
Frankenstein
The Grapes of Wrath
Great Expectations
The Great Gatsby
Gulliver's Travels
Hamlet
Heart of Darkness & The Secret Sharer
Henry IV, Part One
I Know Why the Caged Bird Sings
Iliad
Inferno
Invisible Man
Jane Eyre
Julius Caesar

King Lear
Lord of the Flies
Macbeth
A Midsummer Night's Dream
Moby-Dick
Native Son
Nineteen Eighty-Four
Odyssey
Oedipus Plays
Of Mice and Men
The Old Man and the Sea
Othello
Paradise Lost
A Portrait of the Artist as a Young Man
The Portrait of a Lady

Pride and Prejudice
The Red Badge of Courage
Romeo and Juliet
The Scarlet Letter
Silas Marner
The Sound and the Fury
The Sun Also Rises
A Tale of Two Cities
Tess of the D'Urbervilles
Their Eyes Were Watching God
To Kill a Mockingbird
Uncle Tom's Cabin
Wuthering Heights

COMPREHENSIVE RESEARCH
AND STUDY GUIDE

Langston Hughes

BLOOM'S *MAJOR* POETS

EDITED AND WITH AN INTRODUCTION
BY HAROLD BLOOM

© 1999 by Chelsea House Publishers, a division of Main Line Book Co.

Introduction © 1999 by Harold Bloom

Printed and bound in the United States of America.

3 5 7 9 8 6 4 2

Library of Congress Cataloging-in-Publication Data

Langston Hughes: comprehensive research and study guide / edited and
With an introduction by Harold Bloom.
cm. – (Bloom's major poets)
Includes bibliographical references and index.
ISBN 0-7910-5110-2
Hughes, Langston, 1902-1967—Examinations—Study guides.
2. Hughes, Langston, 1902-1967—Handbooks, manuals, etc.
3. Afro-American poets—20th century—Biography.   4. Afro-Americans
in literature.   I. Bloom, Harold.   II. Series.
PS3515.U274Z716 1998
818'.5209—dc21
98-48532
CIP

Chelsea House Publishers
1974 Sproul Road, Suite 400
Broomall, PA 19008-0914

Contributing Editor: Erica DaCosta

Contents

User's Guide

This volume is designed to present biographical, critical, and bibliographical information on the author's best-known or most important poems. Following Harold Bloom's editor's note and introduction is a detailed biography of the author, discussing major life events and important literary accomplishments. A thematic and structural analysis of each poem follows, tracing significant themes, patterns, and motifs in the work.

A selection of critical extracts, derived from previously published material from leading critics, analyzes aspects of each poem. The extracts consist of statements from the author, if available, early reviews of the work, and later evaluations up to the present. A bibliography of the author's writings (including a complete list of all books written, cowritten, edited, and translated), a list of additional books and articles on the author and the work, and an index of themes and ideas in the author's writings conclude the volume.

~

Harold Bloom is Sterling Professor of the Humanities at Yale University and Henry W. and Albert A. Berg Professor of English at the New York University Graduate School. He is the author of over 20 books and the editor of more than 30 anthologies of literary criticism.

Professor Bloom's works include *Shelley's Mythmaking* (1959), *The Visionary Company* (1961), *Blake's Apocalypse* (1963), *Yeats* (1970), *A Map of Misreading* (1975), *Kabbalah and Criticism* (1975), and *Agon: Toward a Theory of Revisionism* (1982). *The Anxiety of Influence* (1973) sets forth Professor Bloom's provocative theory of the literary relationships between the great writers and their predecessors. His most recent books include *The American Religion* (1992), *The Western Canon* (1994), *Omens of Millennium: The Gnosis of Angels, Dreams, and Resurrection* (1996), and *Shakespeare: The Invention of the Human* (1998).

Professor Bloom earned his Ph.D. from Yale University in 1955 and has served on the Yale faculty since then. He is a 1985 MacArthur Foundation Award recipient and served as the Charles Eliot Norton Professor of Poetry at Harvard University in 1987–88. He is currently the editor of other Chelsea House series in literary criticism, including BLOOM'S NOTES, BLOOM'S MAJOR SHORT STORY WRITERS, MAJOR LITERARY CHARACTERS, MODERN CRITICAL VIEWS, MODERN CRITICAL INTERPRETATIONS, and WOMEN WRITERS OF ENGLISH AND THEIR WORKS.

Editor's Note

My Introduction ventures upon a brief appreciation of the three poems by Langston Hughes that are studied in this volume: "The Weary Blues," "The Negro Speaks of Rivers," and "Song for a Dark Girl."

Hughes's poems, populist and expressionistic, rarely demand, or receive, "close reading." Most of the critical views excerpted in this book tend, therefore, to deal with larger issues. Among the high points are the novelist Richard Wright's praise of Hughes as a forerunner, and James Baldwin's equivocal remarks upon Hughes's *Selected Poems*.

Hughes's definitive scholar-critic-biographer is Arnold Rampersad, whose first excerpt warns us that the poet wore a mask in his "relentless affability and charm." Rampersad is equally perceptive on the origins of Hughes's versions of the blues and the gospel chants, and on the unique amalgam that is constituted by Hughes's life, example, and sophisticated mode of folk poetry.

Introduction

HAROLD BLOOM

The historical and cultural importance of Langston Hughes is unassailable. Though a number of African-American poets have developed their art more fully (Robert Hayden, Jay Wright, and Thylias Moss among them), Hughes wrote a populist poetry (like Carl Sandburg's) to serve the needs of a wider audience. Hughes's acknowledged mentors—Sandburg and Paul Laurence Dunbar—had a generous social vision, and a particular sense of the place of poetry in that vision. Something authentic and powerful almost always struggles to break through into adequate form in Hughes's poetry. The struggle makes him perhaps more of a process-poet than a finished craftsman, but the process is large and central, and of value in itself.

"The Weary Blues," a pioneer effort to fuse formal poetry and oral tradition, seems to carry some reference to Hughes's personal isolation: "I got the Weary Blues/And I can't be satisfied." Whatever his sexual orientation (and it remains ambiguous), Hughes chose personal solitude, which is frequently the burden of his lyrics.

"The Negro Speaks of Rivers," possibly Hughes's most famous poem, has a fairly subtle undersong. The "ancient, dusky rivers," as deep as the black soul, become all but identical with the speaker, and yet they are "older than the flow of human blood in human veins." The repetition of "human" marks an origin before our universal condition, of whatever race. What is best (by implication) and oldest in the poet goes back before the Creation-Fall of Christianity, and hints at Hermetic or Gnostic myth. Hughes, a secular poet, possessed a thwarted religious sensibility, which found expression in his love for, and identification with, his people. That identification tended to exclude Christianity, most memorably in the bitter "Song for a Dark Girl" where: "I asked the white Lord Jesus / What was the use of prayer." The "Song"'s conclusion seems to me Hughes's most eloquent lyric moment: "Love is a naked shadow / On a gnarled and naked tree." Realistically, as a representation of a lynching, that is vivid enough, but again there may well be an undersong, prompted by the poetic will that Rampersad has explicated so usefully. Hughes intimates another Gnostic myth, which is that only a shadow, and not the man Jesus, died upon the cross. A naked cross may be an empty one, and the Gnostics insisted that the authentic Jesus mocked at his supposed immolation. Hughes was a very complex person, split between a sophisticated consciousness and a fierce determination to create a popular and simplified poetic art. His own spirituality may have been more esoteric than we imagine. ❀

Biography of
Langston Hughes

(1902–1967)

Langston Hughes was born in Joplin, Missouri, on February 1, 1902, a direct descendant of heroes of the Abolitionist movement. In a way, his life was defined by his position as an outsider of the culture he wrote about in his poetry. An only child, Hughes was of Indian, French, and African heritage, and the name Langston was well-known and highly respected. With his striking good looks and his outgoing nature, he presented himself as a little prince.

Hughes spent his first thirteen years in Lawrence, Kansas, where he lived with his maternal grandmother, Mary Langston. She raised him on stories of her family's ancestors who fought to end slavery. Mary Langston's first husband rode with John Brown to attack the federal arsenal at Harper's Ferry in 1859 and was killed there; her second husband—Hughes's grandfather—recruited soldiers for the 54th and 55th Massachusetts regiments; Hughes's great uncle was the first black American to hold office by popular vote—as clerk of two Ohio townships—after which he became a professor of law at Howard University. Of black folkways, however, Mary Langston was as ignorant as any white person.

Carrie Langston, Hughes's mother, was brought up as a small-town debutante, but by the time her son was born, her family was penniless. And Lawrence, Kansas—founded as a center of abolitionist activity—was a lost Eden. In 1899, Carrie married James Hughes, who was, like herself, of mixed blood; both of his grandfathers were white. James was cold and ambitious and detested the poor, especially the black poor. The marriage did not last long: James ran off to Mexico, where he prospered working for the American-owned Pullman Company. Carrie went to Kansas City to pursue an acting career, leaving Langston with his grandmother. Carrie soon abandoned the theater and married for a second time; Langston remained with his grandmother. Throughout his youth, Langston yearned to be with his mother, but she showed no interest in her son. This need for love and acceptance, brought on by his mother's long absences, overshadowed his life.

Eventually, Langston followed his mother to Cleveland, where he attended Central High, a racially mixed, well-endowed, progressive school. Hughes was enormously popular. He was on the track team, edited the student literary magazine *Belfry Owl*, and despite an interest in Socialism that was fostered by his many Jewish friends, was president of the American Civic Association. It was at Central he read the poetry of Carl Sandburg and Walt Whitman, and it was there he began to publish his own writing. During his second year, Langston's mother left him again and followed her new husband to Chicago, where he had gone looking for work.

After graduating from high school, eager to experience New York—and especially Harlem—Langston attended Columbia University. Columbia proved stifling and unfulfilling for him; he did not return after his freshman year. Harlem, however, was everything he expected and more. The handful of poems he published in the journal *Crisis* had afforded him some recognition; he was welcomed almost immediately by such famous writers of the Harlem Renaissance as W. E. B. Du Bois and Claude McKay; the poet Countee Cullen became a close friend.

Needing the legitimacy a bachelor's degree would provide, Hughes enrolled in Lincoln University, near Philadelphia, Pennsylvania. Before classes began, he sailed to Europe and Africa, working as a messman on several ships. In 1926, at the age of twenty-four, he published his first book of poetry, *The Weary Blues*, which earned him a place at the forefront of the Harlem Renaissance.

In 1932, Hughes joined a group of twenty-two young blacks traveling to Russia to take part in a Soviet-produced film about race relations in America. The production fell through, but he stayed on in Russia for another year before heading back to the United States. In 1937, Hughes traveled to Spain to cover the civil war as a newspaper correspondent for the *Baltimore Afro-American*. Throughout the 1930s he wrote and published steadily.

Although Hughes entertained Communist sympathies, he denied being a member of the Communist Party. In 1953 he was subpoenaed to appear before Senator Joseph McCarthy's committee investigating Communist activity in the United States. Hughes did not perform well. He cooperated with the committee—short of naming names—and afterwards severed his Socialist connections. Black leftists, including Du Bois and the singer and actor Paul Robeson, considered his retreat a betrayal, and denounced him.

Hughes eventually settled in Harlem, but continued to travel. He was published widely and was able to support himself with his writing. He was never financially secure, however, and more often than not, he was penniless. His celebrity was frequently the only mitigating factor between himself and anonymous poverty.

Hughes published sixteen books of poetry, two novels, seven collections of short fiction, two autobiographies, four books of nonfiction, ten books for children, and more than twenty-five plays. He compiled anthologies, wrote librettos, made recordings of his work, and—fluent in both languages—translated Spanish and French poetry into English. His friends and acquaintances were a veritable pantheon of twentieth-century artists, writers, performers, and thinkers. Even so, loneliness plagued him throughout his life; the regard and affection of so many did little to ease his pain. Hughes never married, nor did he form any long attachments with either men or women. In 1967 Hughes died quietly, alone, in a hospital in Harlem. ❀

All information is taken from the definitive, two-volume biography, *The Life of Langston Hughes,* by Arnold Rampersad.

Thematic Analysis of
"The Weary Blues"

In Hughes's essay "The Negro Artist and the Racial Mountain," written when he was twenty-three, he admired the distinctiveness of the "low down folks," a group to whom he was clearly an outsider. Hughes was possessed of a proud, heroic ancestry and was raised to look down on those American blacks who did not take part in the struggle against racism, as his own forebears had done. It was in these "low down folks" that Hughes eventually found his primary resource and most representative subject. He listened to and absorbed the strange, melancholy exuberance from this most burdened and oppressed of the black underclass, people who had the most reason to despair but showed the least evidence of it. He saw that their means for spiritual survival was folklore. In this pivotal essay, Hughes argues for black artists of every medium to learn from and use black folklore in the same way that jazz musicians learn from and use black folk music.

Blues music, the forerunner of jazz, came directly out of the Negro work song. Hughes used this uniquely black art form throughout his poetry. His earliest memories were of listening to blues as a boy in Lawrence, Kansas. Jazz, and specifically the blues, would become a theme central to his body of work.

Hughes's early commitment to "low down folks" was a recognition of their humor, warmth, and poignant generosity. It was also a rejection of the self-hatred and arrogance projected by his father and, to some degree, his mother, both of whom grew up in decidedly non-folk traditions. The exclusionary superiority of his forebears was what Hughes perceived to be the source of his lifelong sense of isolation and loss. Choosing the most downtrodden and their traditions was a way of choosing himself. Their belief in self-assured surrender was surely attractive to someone as unsettled and striving as Hughes. "From the animal tales to the hipsterish urban myth-making, folk tradition has an is-ness. Things are. Things are funny, sad, tragic, tragicomic, bitter, sweet, tender, harsh, awe-inspiring, cynical, otherworldly, worldly—sometimes alternately expressing the conflicting and contradictory qualities; sometimes, expressing the conflicting qualities simultaneously," George Kent writes in the essay "Langston

Hughes and Afro-American Folk and Cultural Tradition." There is hope where, reasonably, there should be none.

Countee Cullen, a major poet of the Harlem Renaissance at the same period as Langston Hughes, criticized him for his preoccupation with things black. When he reviewed Hughes's collection of poems *The Weary Blues* in the black journal *Opportunity* he wrote: "Taken as a group the selections in this book seem one-sided to me. They tend to hurl this poet into the gaping pit that lies before all Negro artists pure and simple. There is too much emphasis here on strictly Negro themes." This was precisely the soil Hughes intended to till. It was fresh ground Hughes was breaking, yet Hughes remained cautious, reluctant to write anything bawdy or objectionable. "He seems to have struck a compromise: a deep pride in, a deep commitment to, the blues tradition in America, tempered by a desire to present a less extreme or offensive face to the public for acceptance, and by the imposed limitations of the publishing establishment. The acceptance that Hughes sought was not only for himself, but for the black oral tradition and it was an acceptance that provided a beat to which his poetic successors would sing more bawdy, violent or extreme verses," writes Steven C. Tracy, in his essay "To the Tune of Those Weary Blues."

In "The Weary Blues," an old black piano player sings to dispel his unhappiness:

> I's gwine to quit ma frownin'
> And put ma troubles on the shelf.

It was not Hughes's weary despair that defined him. In fact it was his buoyant "lifemanship" that allowed him to sing at all.

> Thump, thump, thump, went his foot on the floor.
> He played a few chords then he sang some more—

The piano player brims with pathos and joy. He celebrates only the moment. He knows that the terrifying leap from this moment to the next one can be held off only through song, through the blues.

Though Hughes is considered a social poet, he did not choose to write about racial division in America. Rather, he felt his task was to legitimize black music and the black folk tradition. "The Weary Blues" is the title poem for his first collection of poetry, published in 1926, when he was twenty-four. His recent move to Harlem afforded him an awareness of city life he never had before, having grown up in Kansas and Missouri. The struggle of poor urban blacks gripped his conscience; still, he does not venture often in his poetry to the edges of black life to witness the hostility of white racial oppression. Because it was not the sum of the American black condition, his inward-looking eye is both his strength and his weakness. The glaring fact of overt racism did not hold Hughes's interest. He championed the black man as himself, not the black man in opposition to the white man.

There are, however, clear instances of protest in Hughes's writing. At the end of the decade of the 1920s, when the popularity of Negro music, literature, and dance was waning, Hughes turned his attention to new subjects. The stock market collapsed, bringing the Great Depression, and the plight of black America, already bleak, worsened. In 1931, nine black youths in Scottsboro, Alabama, were unjustly convicted of rape. Hughes responded in 1932 with four poems and a play, collected as *Scottsboro Limited*; he held nothing back:

> Justice is a blind goddess
> To this we blacks are wise
> Her bandage hides two festering sores
> that once perhaps were eyes.

During the Depression, Hughes's writing grew steadily anticapitalist as he saw for himself the black masses at the bottom being ground up in the urban machine that was engineered to create wealth for the few at the top. His third book of poetry, *A New Song*, was published by the International Worker's Order, an international Communist benevolent society, and was filled with social commentary. When anti-Communist sentiment gripped the country, Joseph McCarthy, the Republican Senator from Wisconsin, subpoenaed Hughes to testify before the House Un-American Activities Committee. Unfortunately, because he cooperated with the committee, he was scorned by his liberal and leftist friends and colleagues. Smarting from the pain of pride and rejection, he abandoned social criticism in his work forever.

Blues and black folklore again became the source and subject matter for his work. His refusal to use standard, conventional forms and his open disaffection for the emerging black middle class were his own subtle means of protest.

"Certainly the Shakespearian sonnet would be no mould in which to express life on Beale Street or Lenox Avenue," Hughes wrote. "I am not interested in doing tricks with rhymes. I am interested in reproducing the human soul if I can." Folk material allowed him to juxtapose the victimization with the jubilance of poor blacks, in the context of the collective black "dream deferred."

> I tried to write poems like the songs they sang on Seventh Street—gay songs, because you had to be gay or die; sad songs, because you couldn't help being sad sometimes. But gay or sad, you kept on living and you kept on going. Their songs—those of Seventh Street—had the pulse of the people who keep on going. ❀

Critical Views on
"The Weary Blues"

COUNTEE CULLEN ON THE EMERGENCE OF LANGSTON
HUGHES AS A MAJOR BLACK ARTIST

[One of the leading poets of the Harlem Renaissance,
Countee Cullen (1903–1946) was a contemporary of
Langston Hughes. His poetry collections include *Color*
(1925), *The Black Christ and Other Poems* (1929), and *The
Medea and Some Poems* (1935).]

Here is a poet with whom to reckon, to experience, and here and
there, with that apologetic feeling of presumption that should com-
panion all criticism, to quarrel.

What has always struck me most forcibly in reading Mr. Hughes's
poems has been their utter spontaneity and expression of a unique
personality. This feeling is intensified with the appearance of his
work in concert between the covers of a book. It must be acknowledged at the outset that these poems are peculiarly Mr. Hughes's and
no one's else. I cannot imagine his work as that of any other poet,
not even of any poet of that particular group of which Mr. Hughes is
a member. Of course, a microscopic assiduity might reveal deriva-
tion and influences, but these are weak undercurrents in the flow of
Mr. Hughes's own talent. This poet represents a transcendently
emancipated spirit among a class of young writers whose particular
battle-cry is freedom. With the enthusiasm of a zealot, he pursues
his way, scornful, in subject matter, in photography, and rhythmical
treatment, of whatever obstructions time and tradition have placed
before him. To him it is essential that he be himself. Essential and
commendable surely; yet the thought persists that some of these
poems would have been better had Mr. Hughes held himself a bit in
check. In his admirable introduction to the book, Carl Van Vechten
says the poems have *a highly deceptive air of spontaneous improvisa-
tion.* I do not feel that the air is deceptive.

If I have the least powers of prediction, the first section of this
book, *The Weary Blues*, will be most admired, even if less from
intrinsic poetic worth than because of its dissociation from the tra-
ditionally poetic. Never having been one to think all subjects and

forms proper for poetic consideration, I regard these jazz poems as interlopers in the company of the truly beautiful poems in other sections of the book. They move along with the frenzy and electric heat of a Methodist or Baptist revival meeting, and effect me in much the same manner. The revival meeting excites me, cooling and flushing me with alternate chills and fevers of emotion; so do these poems. But when the storm is over, I wonder if the quiet way of communing is not more spiritual for the God-seeking heart; and in the light of reflection I wonder if jazz poems really belong to that dignified company, that select and austere circle of high literary expression which we call poetry. Surely, when in "Negro Dancers" Mr. Hughes says,

> Me an' ma baby's
> Got two mo' ways,
> Two mo' ways to do de buck!

he voices, in lyrical, thumb-at-nose fashion the happy careless attitude, akin to poetry, that is found in certain types. And certainly he achieves one of his loveliest lyrics in "Young Singer." Thus I find myself straddling a fence. It needs only "The Cat and The Saxophone," however, to knock me over completely on the side of bewilderment, and incredulity. This creation is a *tour de force* of its kind, but is it a poem:

> EVERYBODY
> Half-pint—
> Gin?
> No, make it
> LOVES MY BABY
> corn. You like
> don't you, honey?
> BUT MY BABY . . .

In the face of accomplished fact, I cannot say *This will never do*, but I feel that it ought never to have been done.

But Mr. Hughes can be as fine and as polished as you like, etching his work in calm, quiet lyrics that linger and repeat themselves. Witness "Sea Calm":

> How still,
> How strangely still
> The water is today
> It is not good
> For water
> To be so still that way.

Or take "Suicide's Note":

> The Calm,
> Cool face of the river
> Asked me for a kiss.

Then crown your admiration with "Fantasy in Purple," this imperial swan-song that sounds like the requiem of a dying people:

> Beat the drums of tragedy for me.
> Beat the drums of tragedy and death.
> And let the choir sing a stormy song
> To drown the rattle of my dying breath.
>
> Beat the drums of tragedy for me,
> And let the white violins whir thin and slow,
> But blow one blaring trumpet note of sun
> To go with me to the darkness where I go.

Mr. Hughes is a remarkable poet of the colorful; through all his verses the rainbow riots and dazzles, yet never wearies the eye, although at times it intrigues the brain into astonishment and exaggerated admiration when reading, say something like "Caribbean Sunset."

> God having a hemorrhage,
> Blood coughed across the sky,
> Staining the dark sea red:
> That is sunset in the Caribbean.

Taken as a group the selections in this book seem one-sided to me. They tend to hurl this poet into the gaping pit that lies before all Negro writers, in the confines of which they become racial artists instead of artists pure and simple. There is too much emphasis here on strictly Negro themes; and this is probably an added reason for my coldness toward the jazz poems—they seem to set a too definite limit upon an already limited field.

Dull books cause no schisms, raise no dissensions, create no parties. Much will be said of *The Weary Blues* because it is a definite achievement, and because Mr. Hughes, in his own way, with a first book that cannot be dismissed as merely *promising*, has arrived.

—Countee Cullen, untitled review of *The Weary Blues* in *Opportunity* 4 (March 1926).

RICHARD WRIGHT ON LANGSTON HUGHES'S ROLE IN FREEING AMERICAN LITERARY EXPRESSION

[Richard Wright (1908–1960) is best known for his 1940 novel *Native Son* and his autobiography, *Black Boy* (1945), both of which portray racism in stark, sometimes shocking terms.]

The double role that Langston Hughes has played in the rise of a realistic literature among the Negro people resembles in one phase the role that Theodore Dreiser played in freeing American literary expression from the restrictions of Puritanism. Not that Negro literature was ever Puritanical, but it was timid and vaguely lyrical and folkish. Hughes's early poems, "The Weary Blues" and "Fine Clothes to the Jew," full of irony and urban imagery, were greeted by a large section of the Negro reading public with suspicion and shock when they first appeared in the middle twenties. Since then the realistic position assumed by Hughes has become the dominant outlook of all those Negro writers who have something to say.

The other phase of Hughes's role has been, for the lack of a better term, that of a cultural ambassador. Performing his task quietly and almost casually, he has represented the Negroes' case, in his poems, plays, short stories and novels, at the court of world opinion. On the other hand he has brought the experiences of other nations within the orbit of the Negro writer by his translations from the French, Russian, and Spanish.

How Hughes became this forerunner and ambassador can best be understood in the cameo sequences of his own life that he gives us in his sixth and latest book, *The Big Sea*. Out of his experiences as a seaman, cook, laundry worker, farm helper, busboy, doorman, unemployed worker, have come his writings dealing with black gals who wore red stockings and black men who sang the blues all night and slept like rocks all day.

Unlike the sons and daughters of Negro "society," Hughes was not ashamed of those of his race who had to scuffle for their bread. The jerky transitions of his own life did not admit of his remaining in one place long enough to become a slave of prevailing Negro middle-class prejudices. So beneficial does this ceaseless movement seem to Hughes that he has made it one of his life principles: six months in one place, he says, is long enough to make one's life complicated. The result has been a range of artistic interest and expression possessed by no other Negro writer of his time.

—Richard Wright, "Forerunner and Ambassador" (review of *The Big Sea*) in *The New Republic* 103 (October 1940).

GEORGE KENT ON HUGHES'S EXPERIMENTATION WITH BLUES MUSIC AND THE USE OF RELIGIOUS TRADITION

[George E. Kent taught Afro-American literature at the University of Chicago. He is the author of *Blackness and the Adventure of Western Civilization* (1972).]

I would tentatively say that Hughes is best when he attempts to capture the blues spirit and varied forms of response to existence in a poem that uses non-blues devices. Among such poems would be "Reverie on the Harlem River," "Early Evening Quarrel," "Mama and Daughter," and especially, "Lover's Return." Such poems can combine the simplicities of free verse, the free dramatizing of concrete situations, the folk tendency to hold in suspension contradictory attitudes, the incisive folk definition, and various formal resources of literary technique, for the effective rendering that is more available to the self-conscious and relatively isolated artist.

In an overall way, it may also be said that Hughes gains a good deal from experimentation with blues form. One certainly could not imagine his having to buy a Bessie Smith record, as James Baldwin reports that he once did, in order to get back to how blacks actually express themselves or to recapture the sound patterns of their speech. Hughes seldom strikes a false note with black sound patterns, and these are apparent also in non-blues poems. His poems are also full of the hard complex attitudes of the people stubbornly "on the go," whom he mentions in his autobiography, *The Big Sea*. He is seldom at the mercy of forms that immediately evoke experiences whose essentials are not those of the black experience, a dilemma that sometimes catches up with Claude McKay as we hear him crowded by the romantic tradition and the sudden notes of Byron or Shelley.

It is, of course, possible to credit too much to his contact with a single form, and to overlook the fact that Hughes was drawing from the whole of black culture. Suffice it to say that the self confronting defiantly the enemy at home and abroad is amply evident in his blues and blues-toned poems.

There is evidence in Hughes's poetry of his capturing the forms of response of the fold implied by the religious tradition and its cultural modes of expression: the spirituals, gospel songs, and the sermon. In most of such poems the concentration is not on the close duplication of form that is sometimes encountered in the blues poems, but upon mood, definitions, motifs, and the determination and persistence provided by having a friend not made of earth. Such approaches to life can sometimes be rendered through dramatization of personalities who sometimes mention God—but not always. Such poems as "Aunt Sue's Stories," "The Negro Mother," "Mother to Son," and even the poem that strikes the blues note, "Stony Lonesome," convey a sense of standing erect upon the earth by means of a quiet but deep relationship to something more than this world.

Perhaps the closest that Hughes came to attempting to catch the immediate bounce and beat of a form is the emphasis upon the gospel music form and beat found in the poem, "Fire," which begins:

> Fire,
> Fire, Lord!
> Fire gonna burn ma soul!

The beat of the gospel music can be heard, and if one has been exposed to the musical accompaniment, it too can be heard. But it is only necessary to read a few gospel songs or to hear Mahalia Jackson render one in the ecstatic modulations that have made her famous to realize that Hughes is trying neither to mount to the heights nor to give the typical resolution of conflict that is usually essential to the form. In the spiritual tradition, Hughes is better at rendering the quieter moments, even when they involve desperation, which may be found in such poems as "Sinner," "Litany," "Feet of Jesus," and "Judgment Day," although he can mount to the ecstatic by combining well-established lines and images drawn from tradition with other literary resources as he does in "Spirituals."

Hughes's spectacular effort in the vein of the folk sermon is "Sunday Morning Prophecy," but he makes no effort to exploit the full sermon form: the conventional apology for ineptitude, the clear statement and explanation of text, and the movement into ecstatic seizure by the spirit. The ecstatic seizure and eloquent imagery characteristic of the folk sermon are utilized, but the emphasis is finally upon the powerful condemnation of things of this world and the minister's final plea:

> Come into the church this morning,
> Brothers and Sisters,
> And be saved—
> And give freely
> In the collection basket
> That I who am thy shepherd
> Might live.
>
> Amen!

—George E. Kent, "Hughes and the Afro-American Folk and Cultural Tradition," in *Blackness and the Adventure of Western Culture* (Chicago: Third World Press, 1972).

ONWUCHEKWA JEMIE ON JAZZ POETRY

[Onwuchekwa Jemie is the author of *Langston Hughes: An Introduction to the Poetry* (1973).]

Jazz poetry might be viewed as a stage in that search for native American rhythms begun by Walt Whitman and carried forward in the early twentieth century by such poets as Vachel Lindsay and Carl Sandburg. Its ancestor on the black side is the dialect poetry of Paul Laurence Dunbar, which was built on black speech rhythms of the rural South. Of Hughes's contemporaries, Lindsay especially had established a reputation as a jazz poet with his "General William Booth Enters into Heaven" (1913), a rhythmic adaptation of black folk sermons, with built-in leader-choral antiphony and the accompaniment of drums, banjos, flutes, and tambourines; and with his racist "The Congo: A Study of the Negro Race" (1914), which came with precise marginal notes on mood and musical accompaniment. "The Congo" is a rehearsal of fantastic events in black lands of the white imagination, and a panegyric on the white man's so-called "civilizing mission" in Africa.

> THEN I had religion, THEN I had a vision.
> I could not turn from their revel in derision.
> THEN I SAW THE CONGO, CREEPING THROUGH THE BLACK,
> CUTTING THROUGH THE FOREST WITH A GOLDEN
>   TRACK. . . .

> "Be careful what you do,
> Or Mumbo-Jumbo, God of the Congo . . .
> Mumbo-Jumbo will hoo-doo you,
> Mumbo-Jumbo will hoo-doo you,
> Mumbo-Jumbo will hoo-doo you. . . .

> Boomlay, boomlay, boomlay, boom.
> Boomlay, boomlay, boomlay, boom.
> Boomlay, boomlay, boomlay, boom
> Boomlay, boomlay, boomlay,
> BOOM."

Much of the poem's strength is in its rhythmic energy, its repetitions and imitative sounds, the vivid detail in which the varied scenes are painted, and the terror of the experience which is so vitally captured and dramatized. In his ability to recount the experience, Lindsay's spiritual voyager is Coleridge's Ancient Mariner, Sinbad the Sailor, and a convert testifying at a Holy Roller church all in one. Hughes himself has acknowledged the debt he owes to Dunbar, Sandburg, and Lindsay, among others. His "Song for a Banjo Dance" could be read as a version of Dunbar's "A Negro Love Song." His "Harlem Night Club" and "Jazz Band in a Parisian Cabaret" remind us of Sandburg's "Jazz Fantasia" (1920). And his *Ask Your Mama* is closely related in form and manner to Lindsay's "The Congo."

Dunbar's dialect poetry, and the dialect stories of Charles Waddell Chesnutt, together constituted the fullest flowering in black literature of a nineteenth-century tradition which was popularized by the white minstrel stage and by white writers of the Southern local color school such as George Washington Cable, Thomas Nelson Page, Joel Chandler Harris, and Irwin Russell. Both Chesnutt and Dunbar attempted to turn dialect inside out, to purge it of its all too familiar stereotypes of the happy-go-lucky, chicken-stealing, comic Sambo, but with limited success (with Dunbar the less successful). Chesnutt's last published novel in 1905, and Dunbar's death in 1906, might be said to have brought to a close the nineteenth century in black literature. The next fifteen to twenty years saw a dramatic shift in black population from the rural South to the urban North; and as it turned out, the transition in literature from nineteenth to twentieth century, and from dialect poetry to jazz poetry and blues, paralleled that Great Migration. As might be expected, the younger generation of writers took their cues from Dunbar and Chesnutt, but they soon discovered that dialect was too old and crumbly to survive a face lift. It was impossible to use dialect and avoid the stereotypes. But fortunately for them, their coming of age coincided with the boisterous jazz and blues age, and it was in the contemporary life, language, and music of the city, rather than in the South and the past, that they found what James Weldon Johnson has called "form[s] that will express the racial spirit by symbols from within rather than by symbols from without (such as the mere mutilation of English spelling and pronunciation)."

The jazz poem was such a form; and while Hughes did not invent it, he carried it to a high level of development. He manages to suggest the frenetic energy of instrumental jazz in the breathless enumerations of "Railroad Avenue," "Jitney," "Man into Men," "Brass Spittoons," and "Laughers," and the complex interplay of instruments in the counterpoint of voices in "Mulatto," "Closing Time," and "The Cat and the Saxophone":

EVERYBODY
Half-pint,—
Gin?
No, make it
LOVES MY BABY
corn. You like
liquor,
don't you, honey?
BUT MY BABY
Sure. Kiss me,
DON'T LOVE NOBODY
daddy.
BUT ME.
Say!
EVERYBODY
Yes?
WANTS MY BABY
I'm your

BUT MY BABY
sweetie, ain't I?
DON'T WANT NOBODY
Sure.
BUT
Then let's
ME,
do it!
SWEET ME.
Charleston,
Mamma!
!

Of "The Cat and the Saxophone" Countee Cullen wrote: "This creation is a *tour de force* of its kind, but is it a poem?"—a question not to be asked.

—Onwuchekwa Jemie, *Langston Hughes: An Introduction to the Poetry* (New York: Columbia University Press, 1973).

ROGER ROSENBLATT ON THE INFLUENCE OF JAZZ IN *NOT WITHOUT LAUGHTER*

[Roger Rosenblatt, formerly literary editor of *The New Republic*, is the author of *Black Fiction* (1974).]

Sandy gets his music from the blues which Jimboy and Harriet sing and dance to. Music in *Not without Laughter* functions partly as a narcotic, but each of the songs in the book, like the original slave songs, contains a sober or practical undercurrent. Occasionally the music gets out of control, and the undercurrent overwhelms the sound. At the dance Harriet attends, the four black men in "Benbow's wandering band" were

> exploring depths to which mere sound had no business to go.
> Cruel, desolate, unadorned was their music now, like the body
> of a ravished woman on the sun-baked earth; violent and hard,
> like a giant standing over his bleeding mate in the blazing sun.
> The odors of bodies, the stings of flesh, and the utter emptiness
> of soul when all is done—these things the piano and the drums,

> the cornet and the twanging banjo insisted on hoarsely to a beat
> that made the dancers move, in that little hall, like pawns on a
> frenetic checker board.

The music is described in similes of violence and fate, both of which usually play beneath the surface of blues lyrics, and which attend Jimboy's and Harriet's lives throughout the story. Sandy merely listens pleased to the music around him, and does not participate in it, but in the first pages of the book, Hughes hints at the more sinister effects of music on the boy. In the wake of the opening hurricane, "Sandy saw a piano flat on its back in the grass. Its ivory keys gleamed in the moonlight like grinning teeth, and the strange sight made his little body shiver."

Laughter, the third force which operates on Sandy, is the most conspicuous and consistent of the three. There is always a great deal of laughing going on in this novel, Jimboy's and Harriet's especially. Harriet's boyfriend is described in terms of his grin; Maudel, the town madame, is forever laughing; during the dance "a ribbon of laughter swirled a round the hall." There is much ridiculous activity in the story as well, particularly the absurd projects of Hager's church, which presents a pageant called "The Drill of All Nations," in which Anjee plays Sweden. Laughter is also connected with music, as in the image of the grinning piano. In Hughes's description of the band, the banjo is cynical, the drums are flippant, and the cornet laughs.

The reason for this connection is that both laughter and music are instruments of desolation in the novel, the more so for their conventional and hypothetical associations with joy. The townspeople's amusement at the antics of the freaks in the carnival is hollow and mirthless, as was the reaction of the audience to the boxing dwarfs in *Cane*. Here, as in *Cane*, as in Eliot's "Hysteria," there is a fierce desperation behind everything which is theoretically funny. Jimboy finds momentary companionship with the carnival's Fat Lady because he knows that in another context he too is a freak. He also senses that he and Sandy in the audience have a kinship with the act they watch: Sambo and Rastus, "the world's funniest comedians," who perform on a plantation set accompanied by women in bandanas singing "longingly about Dixie." Sambo and Rastus go though their act with wooden razors and dice as their props. They argue over money until a ghost suddenly appears and scares the two of them away. This the white audience finds "screamingly funny—and just like niggers." The act ends with a black banjo player picking the blues; "to Sandy it seemed like the saddest music in the world—but the white people around him laughed."

—Roger Rosenblatt, *Black Fiction* (Cambridge, Mass.: Harvard University Press, 1974).

CHIDI IKONNE ON THE NARRATIVE STYLE OF "THE WEARY BLUES"

[Chidi Ikonne is assistant professor and acting chairman of Afro-American Studies at Harvard University. He is the author of *From DuBois to Van Vechten: The Early New Negro Literature 1903–1926* (1982).]

Langston Hughes and his associates were not the first Afro-Americans to apply folk treatment to Negro folk material. James Edwin Campbell, Paul Laurence Dunbar, Daniel Webster Davis, J. Mord Allen, the early James Weldon Johnson, and many others had written about the "common [black] elements" in Negro dialect. Not all their works, however, anticipated the self-pride and self-expression of the Harlem Renaissance literature. Many of them belonged to the minstrel tradition. In many cases, although their subject looked black and their language of creation supposedly was Negro, their end product lacked the Negro soul. Created purposely for the delectation of the white folk whose self-aggrandizement they also sought to sustain, these earlier works comprised mainly those Negro elements which experience had proved to be pleasurable to the white ego. They were, essentially, attempts to recreate the white man's concept of the black man. In other words, the Negro artists often borrowed their black material from the white man's imagination. With regard to their form, the dialect (folk) poems most often differed from their literary counterparts only in orthography. In some cases their folk treatment did not go beyond a distortion of English syntax.

Consequently, when Langston Hughes arrived on the scene the process he was to adopt was almost nonexistent, even though some critics confused it with the old minstrel tradition and feared that it might cater to the old self-aggrandizement of the white folk. Drawing his subjects straight form real (as distinct from imagined) Negro folks, he experimented with the blues and jazz forms and employed the real dialect of real Negroes, mainly of Washington, D.C., Harlem, and the South Side, Chicago. Among the results of his first experiments are "The Weary Blues," "Jazzonia," and "Negro Dancers"—poems which are important not only because they are three of his best, but also because they were the very ones that he showed to Vachel Lindsay at the Wardman Park Hotel, Washington, D.C., in December 1925. They set the tone for much of Langston Hughes's later poetry; as such they deserve a closer look.

Thomas Millard Henry was not completely wrong when he applied the phrase "a little story of action and life" to "The Weary Blues," which earned Hughes the forty-dollar first prize in the poetry section of *Opportunity*'s 1925 contest. An attempt to paint a folk creator of the blues in the very action of creation, the poem is essentially a process analysis, a rhetorical pattern which is very close to narrative. Its title notwithstanding, it is hardly a true imitation of the folk blues—a genre which James Weldon Johnson rightly described as a "repository of folk-poetry." At least its form does not agree with the description of the blues pattern as given by Langston Hughes himself in 1927:

> The *Blues*, unlike the *Spirituals*, have a strict poetic pattern: one long line repeated and a third line to rhyme with the first two. Sometimes the second line in repetition is slightly changed and sometimes, but very seldom, it is omitted. The mood of the *Blues* is almost always despondency, but when they are sung people laugh.

Yet "The Weary Blues" is a successful poem. The monotonous, and therefore boring, sentence patterns with very little or no attention to syntax combine with the folk artist's "droning," "rocking," and swaying as well as the implication of the "old gas light," the "poor piano," and the "rickety stool" to underscore the dreariness of the player's life. We feel his blues-infected soul not only in the "sad raggy tune" squeezed out of the "poor" moaning piano, or in the "drowsy syncopated tune" and "mellow croon," but also in his helplessness vis-à-vis the song which rises in him and overflows, almost unaided, his tired voice in the semi-darkness of "an old gas light." The mood is that of "despondency." It is the mood of blues, an art form which Hughes thought was more dolorous than the spirituals because its sorrow is untempered by tears but intensified by an existentialistic laughter.

With regard to its coming too close to being an ordinary narrative, "a little story of action and life," it is even doubtful that it could have done otherwise, since the blues as a poetic expression is an exposé of an active experience physically lived through, or being contemplated mentally or internally ongoing.

—Chidi Ikonne, *From DuBois to Van Vechten: The Early New Negro Literature, 1903-1926* (New York: Greenwood Press, 1981).

STEVEN TRACY ON HUGHES'S EARLY JAZZ AND BLUES EXPERIENCES

[Stephen Tracy lives and works in Cincinnati. He is the author of *Langston Hughes and the Blues* and *Going to Cincinnati: A History of the Blues in the Queen City*.]

In his autobiography *The Big Sea*, Hughes discusses his birth in 1902 in Joplin, Missouri, and his childhood in Lawrence, Kansas, recounting the fact that he heard the blues in the area where he grew up until about 1915. According to Hughes, the first blues song he heard was used in his poem "The Weary Blues," written about a piano player he heard in Harlem:

> I got the weary blues
> And I can't be satisfied.
> Got the weary blues
> And can't be satisfied.
> I ain't happy no mo'
> And I wish that I had died.

The lyric, of course, is formulaic: the formula is repeated with many minor variations in the oral blues tradition, as by Texas songster Henry Thomas whose "Texas Worried Blues" makes the common substitution of "worried" for "weary";

The worried blues
God, I'm feelin' bad.
I've got the worried blues
God, I'm feelin' bad.
I've got the worried blues
God, I'm feelin' bad.

Thomas, who was around fifty-three years old when he first recorded in 1927, represents a link to pre-war blues music, and his blues were often primitive. Hence he characteristically repeats the same three line three times, as opposed to creating a third-line resolution, as younger bluesmen have done.

The ballads, reels and crude blues of an older man like Henry Thomas, that Hughes first heard in his Lawrence childhood from 1902–1915, were his earlier musical influence; therefore it is important to place that tradition in order to discern the type of the music. Lawrence is in northeast Kansas on the Kansas River, approximately sixty miles west of Kansas City, connected by highways 69 and 70 and the Santa Fe, Rock Island, and Missouri-Kansas-Texas railways to Oklahoma, Missouri, Kansas and Texas. Indeed Henry Thomas at a 1929 recording session, recounted his experience hopping the Texas and Pacific and "Katy" (MKT) lines in his "Railroading Some," going from Texas through Kansas City and on through to Chicago, following a route that had been open to passengers, migrants and hoboes for years. The blues were indeed no newcomer to the area: it was in Kansas City in 1902 (the date of Hughes's birth) that blues singer Gertrude "Ma" Rainey reportedly first heard blues music, and Kansas City blues shouter Big Joe Turner, roughly a contemporary of Hughes, recalled leading around blues singers on the streets in the late teens and early twenties, and hearing the crude banjos, gas pipes, and water jugs that were used as instruments. These early blues, often sung unaccompanied, or accompanied by a guitar, piano, or crude home instruments were, in Kansas City, set in a milieu of varied musical idioms—ragtime, jazz, orchestral music—which produced the "loose, lithe, resilient orchestral jazz style to which the city gives its name." This orchestral-type blues were emerging in the teens, flowering in the era of 1925–42, when larger ensembles touring the southwest played blues in arranged form. Thus, during his childhood and visits back home, Hughes was hearing not only "pure" loosely arranged, spontaneous early blues, but most likely these other idioms and various combinations of a more arranged and sophisticated nature. What ultimately emerged in 1925–42 was the ensemble Kansas City blues style, "big city blues, but with a country, earthy feeling," that helped produce or catapult to success Big Joe Turner, Peter Johnson, Jay McShann, Mary Lou Williams, and Count Basie, among others.

But it was the early blues of itinerant musicians of the first two decades of the twentieth century that influenced Hughes in his Lawrence, Kansas, days and the blues of that area were strongly influenced by slave and work songs. The Texas blues scene is more readily identifiable than that of Kansas, Missouri, or other surrounding states because more record companies held sessions in Texas, whereas only the Okeh Record Company recorded sessions in Kansas City. However, the highways and train lines provided easily accessible connections to Kansas, so it is not hard to imagine someone like Texan Willard "Ramblin" Thomas rambling in Kansas singing:

> Poor Boy
> Poor Boy
> Poor Boy long ways from home.

—Stephen Tracy, "To the Tune of Those Weary Blues: The Influence of the Blues Tradition in Langston Hughes's Blues Poems," *MELUS* 8 (1981).

R. BAXTER MILLER ON HUGHES'S DIVERSE TECHNIQUE IN "THE WEARY BLUES"

[R. Baxter Miller is professor of English and director of the Black Literature Program at the University of Tennessee, Knoxville. He is the author of *Langston Hughes and Gwendolyn Brooks: A Reference Guide* and *For a Moment I Wondered: The Literary Imagination of Langston Hughes* (1986).]

A broad overview of *The Weary Blues* clarifies the thematic unity and diverse technique. Grouped according to seven romantic ideas, sixty-eight poems appear under seven headings. While the emphasis goes to the collective consciousness derived from African ancestry in particular and human history in general, other concerns are personal loneliness, isolation, and loss. Still signifying the Harlem Renaissance and the Jazz Age, a third set presents the cabarets, infusing interracial sex within overtones of the exotic. In a deftness often overlooked, Hughes uses anaphora to narrate an imperial self so as to sustain the blues stanza as countermelody and ironic understatement. What most complements the lyric skill concerns the dramatic movement of feeling. Through the impulse, he portrays the child's maturation into the state of the lost imagination and the transmutation of suffering into art. In narrative distancing his speakers achieve a double identification. While they situate themselves in the dramatic situation implied, they share the reader's historical consciousness. The lyric hardly represents all of the range, but the formal movement does counterplay to the dramatic tragedy suggested.

Indeed, the performance in the title poem completes the ritualistic conversion from Black American suffering into epic communion. On 1 May 1925, during a banquet at an "elegant" Fifth Avenue restaurant in New York City, the poem won a prize from *Opportunity* magazine, where it subsequently appeared. The thirty-five-line lyric presents a singer who plays one night on Harlem's Lenox Avenue. Having performed well in the club, the pianist goes to bed, as the song still sounds in the mind. In the dull pallor, and beneath the old gas light, he has played his ebony hands on the ivory keys. During the "lazy sway" from the bar stool, he has patted the floor with his feet, done a few chords, and then sung some more. Finally, he sleeps "like a rock that's dead," the artistic spirit exhausted.

His performance clearly implies several dramatic actions. While one sets the dynamic playing, the black self-affirmation against what fades, a second concerns a vital remaking of the Black self-image. A third shows the transcendence through racial stereotype into lyrical style. From the dramatic situation of the player, both musical as well as performed, the poem imposes the isolation and loneliness, yet the refusal to accept them. The song marks a metonym for the human imagination.

When Hughes's speakers step back from the dramatic performance into the lyric perception, they delimit the space of dream, sometimes in covertly sexual metaphor. At the detached distance from any dramatic situation, they even remake the iconography of

Black and White, often revising and neutralizing the traditional code of culture, race, and value. Written in two stanzas, "Dream Variations" has nine lines in the first part and eight in the second one. While the persona longs for his dream, he sees the externalization in Nature, the place and the sun. What confronts him concerns the very duality of dream, which exists only in the lyric moment of timelessness. For the player within the concealed story, on the night in 1924, the performance must be completed in time to assure the customary paycheck.

—R. Baxter Miller, *The Art and Imagination of Langston Hughes* (Lexington: University Press of Kentucky, 1986).

C. James Trotman on "The Negro Artist and the Racial Mountain"

[C. James Trotman is professor of English at West Chester University.]

"The Negro Artist and the Racial Mountain" was such an early place for Hughes. An imaginary lookout post, a lighthouse of sorts, this essay first appeared in the *Nation* in 1926. It was an artistic manifesto in which Hughes voiced the independent integrity of the black artist, an important concept at any time but historically representative of the *zeitgeist* of this century's first quarter. This was a tumultuous epoch roaring with revolutionary militancy from Petrograd and Paris to the Negro Renaissance in America. Moreover, the image of the artist standing almost, but not quite existentially, aloof on a peak with racial markers, embraces so many of our impressions and understanding about creative artists, their works, and our responses to them. The fusion of experiences and devices of art, the imaginative uses of facts and fictions, the private and public wanderings are well-known scenes in the artist's *rite de passage*. When thinking about Hughes's life, his work, and his influence in this context, we begin another celebrated journey. Part of his drawing power as a belletrist is to be found in the variety of these sojourns.

Hughes was a peripatetic artist. On a global scale, his own international travels began in 1923 when he went to Africa and, later, to Europe in the same year. As readers we are drawn with him into symbolic, ancestral reflections in "The Negro Speaks of Rivers" (1921) and into autobiographical accounts of these travels recorded later in *The Big Sea* (1940). Sounds, particularly the musical quality of words, pulled him into the cultural repository of African American music where he used the blues for lyric poetry. In doing so, he expanded the American prosodic expression by incorporating this expressive folk form into the distinctive collection of poetry. But far more fundamental to Hughes's art was that language was a creative source for drawing with exquisite clarity and compassion the lives, manners, and customs of black folk.

—C. James Trotman, *Langston Hughes, The Man, His Art, and His Continuing Influence* (New York/London: Garland Publishing, 1995).

CHERYL WALL ON HUGHES AND BESSIE SMITH

[Cheryl A. Wall is associate professor of English at Rutgers University.]

Langston Hughes was, characteristically, prescient in his understanding of the blues women's significance. As one imperative of his artistic manifesto, "The Negro Artist and the Racial Mountain," declared: "Let the blare of Negro jazz bands and the bellowing voice of Bessie Smith singing Blues penetrate the closed ears of the colored near-intellectuals until they listen and perhaps understand." Not only was Hughes drawn to the compressed poetry of the blues, he aspired to a cultural role analogous to the blues troubadour. Fittingly, he was a student and admirer of the blues woman's art.

In 1926 Hughes made his pilgrimage to the Empress's domain. Bessie Smith was appearing at the Regent Theater in Baltimore when the author of the just published *The Weary Blues* made his way backstage to pay his respects. Doubtless he knew her recording "Mama's Got the Blues," which began "Some people say the weary blues ain't bad." Perhaps he hoped for recognition as a fellow blues artist.

According to Hughes's biographer, Arnold Rampersad, whatever such aspirations he held were dashed. Miss Smith was not impressed. Hughes was disappointed in turn when he asked whether she had a theory about blues as Art: "Naw, she didn't know nothing about no art. All she knew was that blues had put her 'in de money.'"

Whether she chose to theorize about it or not, Hughes understood that Bessie Smith knew a great deal about art. He understood as well that her life, and the lives of the other blues queens, could be the stuff of fiction. In his 1930 novel, *Not Without Laughter*, Hughes became the first writer to represent the figure of the blues woman in literature. His character Harriett Williams should be considered a precursor to the memorable blues women invented by Alice Walker in *The Color Purple*, Toni Cade Bambara in "Medley," and Sherley Anne Williams in *Someone Sweet Angel Chile*.

—Cheryl A. Wall, *Langston Hughes, The Man, His Art, and His Continuing Influence* (New York/London: Garland Publishing, 1995).

Thematic Analysis of
"The Negro Speaks of Rivers"

Langston Hughes published "The Negro Speaks of Rivers" in *The Crisis*, the most important journal of black life, in June 1921; with this his career began. He quickly rose to prominence during the Harlem Renaissance of the 1920s, when American black writers, musicians, and artists began to be recognized. With the Depression, however, his financial opportunities diminished, and he had to think about being able to support himself as a writer:

> I wanted to continue to be a poet. Yet sometimes I wondered if I was barking up the wrong tree. I determined to find out by taking poetry, my poetry, to my people. After all, I wrote about Negroes, and primarily for Negroes. Would they hate me? Did they want me? (Langston Hughes, *I Wonder As I Wander*)

Hughes appropriated black folk traditions, tales, and music and used them as the basis for his art, but he never lost sight of their American context. To be both black and American was to him a condition of fundamental disunity: It was two separate identities that lived in contention within the same soul. W. E. B. Du Bois wrote about this condition in *The Souls of Black Folk:*

> It is a peculiar sensation, this double-consciousness, this sense of always looking at oneself through the eyes of others, of measuring one's soul by the tape of a world that looks on in amused contempt and pity. One ever feels his twoness—an American, a Negro; two souls, two thoughts, two unreconciled strivings; two warring ideals in one body, whose dogged strength alone keeps it from being torn asunder.

For Hughes, the duality was sharper and more complex even than this, because he was not entirely a part of the people for whom he wrote. His family was an arrogant, ambitious lot who moved in white circles, went to white schools, and especially in the case of his father, looked down on lower-class blacks. In his first autobiography, *The Big Sea*, Hughes describes an exchange with his father that took place one summer in his youth; the dialogue tells of a rift much deeper than the usual conflicts between fathers and sons:

> "What do you want to be?"
> "I don't know. But I think a writer."

"A writer?" my father said. "A writer? . . . Do they make any money? . . . Learn something you can make a living from anywhere in the world, in Europe or South America, and don't stay in the States, where you have to live like a nigger with niggers."

"But I like Negroes," I said.

Both his father's and Langston's own sense of otherness are evident here. Although one has contempt for and the other has fondness for American blacks, both view them as outsiders. Langston's mixed blood and his family's hostility toward oppressed, undereducated blacks made his "black American dilemma" a problem without solutions.

When Hughes gave a lecture tour in the South in the summer of 1931, he was—unfortunately—at last—exposed to the full force of American bigotry. "I found a great social and cultural gulf between the races in the South, astonishing to one who, like myself, from the North, had never known such uncompromising prejudices." His black consciousness grew and solidified during this period, yet his sense of alienation was heightened as well, as he faced these southern blacks who were forced into a kind of submission he himself had never fully known.

Hughes raises the issue of his own mixed origins in his poem "Cross":

> My old man died in a fine big house.
> My ma died in a shack.
> I wonder where I'm gonna die,
> Being neither white nor black?

This uncharacteristically bitter sense of his own racial otherness evidences a certain insecurity and provides a glimpse into his strong, lifelong struggle to be accepted.

The difficulties in the duality of being black in America are overcome in the poem "I, Too, Sing America." Hughes here is proud of both his black and American identities.

> I am the darker brother.
> They send me to eat in the kitchen
> When company comes,
> But I laugh,
> And eat well,
> And grow strong.

Hughes portrays the black American experience most successfully in five collections of short stories with his character Jesse B. Semple, the exemplar of Hughes's beloved "low-down folks." Hughes crystalizes the black American predicament through conversations and arguments between Semple and Semple's friend Boyd. Although he is black, Boyd is a romantic idealist who refuses to place any importance on race; Semple is the realist: "Negroes today are . . . advancing, advancing!" insists Boyd. Semple responds, "I have not advanced one step, still the same old job, same old salary, same old kitchenette, same old Harlem and the same old color." Boyd, the assimilated black man, confronts Semple, the unalloyed black man; there is no resolution.

Hughes strove for a selfhood that was both artless and wise. In "The Negro Speaks of Rivers," the references to Africa evoke this quality of both simplicity and guilelessness. Although the poem projects an overtly romantic vision of African primitivism, primitivism itself was not the focus of Hughes's attention. Africa is simultaneously a symbol of the black self and a symbol of all men. Human consciousness, not only black consciousness, finds its roots in east Africa. The waters of the rivers of Africa mingle with that of the Mississippi. Human history exists everywhere at once, from the dawn of man to the edge of the Harlem Renaissance. To have "known rivers" is to have known what it is to be a man in the world.

After a harrowing trip down the Congo in his twenties, Hughes's view of Africa matured, but he continued to use African references to celebrate and affirm the black self. Nevertheless, his sense of individuality was unable to mitigate his sense of solitude, his sense of exclusion, as expressed so poignantly and innocently in his poem "Dream Variations":

> To fling my arms wide
> In some place of the sun,
> To whirl and to dance
> Till the white day is done.
> Then rest at cool evening
> Beneath a tall tree
> While night comes on gently,
>   Dark like me—
> That is my dream!
>
> To fling my arms wide
> In the face of the sun,
> Dance! Whirl! Whirl!
> Till the quick day is done.
> Rest at pale evening . . .
> A tall slim tree . . .
> Night coming tenderly
>   Black like me. ❀

Critical Views on
"The Negro Speaks of Rivers"

JAMES BALDWIN ON "SELECTED POEMS"

[An African-American novelist and essayist, James Baldwin (1924–1987) is best known for his novel *Go Tell It on the Mountain* (1953) and the essay *The Fire Next Time* (1963).]

Every time I read Langston Hughes I am amazed all over again by his genuine gifts and depressed that he has done so little with them. A real discussion of this work demands more space than I have here, but this book contains a great deal which a more disciplined poet would have thrown into the wastebasket (almost all of the last section, for example).

There are the poems which almost succeed but which do not succeed, poems which take refuge, finally, in a fake simplicity in order to avoid the very difficult simplicity of the experience! And one sometimes has the impression, as in a poem like "Third Degree"—which is about the beating up of a Negro boy in a police station—that Hughes has had to hold the experience outside him in order to be able to write at all. And certainly this is understandable. Nevertheless, the poetic trick, so to speak, is to be within the experience and outside it at the same time—and the poem fails.

Mr. Hughes is at his best in brief, sardonic asides, or in lyrics like "Mother to Son," and "The Negro Speaks of Rivers." Or "Dream Variations":

> To fling my arms wide
> In some place of the sun,
> To whirl and to dance
> Till the white day is done.
> Then rest at cool evening
> Beneath a tall tree
> While night comes on gently,
>   Dark like me—
> That is my dream!
>
> To fling my arms wide
> In the face of the sun.

Dance! Whirl! Whirl!
Till the quick day is done.
Rest at pale evening ...
A tall, slim tree ...
Night coming tenderly
   Black like me.

I do not like all of "The Weary Blues," which copies, rather than exploits, the cadence of the blues, but it comes to a remarkable end. And I am also fond of "Island," which begins "Wave of sorrow / Do not drown me now."

Hughes, in his sermons, blues and prayers, has working for him the power and the beat of Negro speech and Negro music. Negro speech is vivid largely because it is private. It is a kind of emotional shorthand—or sleight-of-hand—by means of which Negroes express, not only their relationship to each other, but their judgment of the white world. And as the white world takes over this vocabulary—without the faintest notion of what it really means—the vocabulary is forced to change. The same thing is true of Negro music which has had to become more and more complex in order to continue to express any of the private or collective experience.

Hughes knows the bitter truth behind these hieroglyphics, what they are designed to convey. But he has not forced them into the realm of art where their meaning would become clear and over-whelming. "He, pop / Re-bop! / Mop" conveys much more on Lenox Avenue than it does in this book, which is not the way it ought to be.

Hughes is an American Negro poet and has no choice but to be acutely aware of it. He is not the first American Negro to find the war between his social and artistic responsibilities all but irreconcilable.

—James Baldwin, *Selected Poems of Langston Hughes* (New York: Alfred A. Knopf, 1959).

Raymond Smith on Major Influences in Hughes's Poetry

[Raymond Smith writes on American culture. In this essay, he notes how Hughes's childhood memories had as much influence on his poetic style as did other poets.]

Though he did credit Dunbar and Sandburg among his influences, these literary mentors pale in light of what Hughes had to say about his method of poem-writing: "Generally, the first two or three lines come to me from something I'm thinking about, or looking at, or doing, and the rest of the poem (if there is to be a poem) flows from those first few lines, usually right away." This spontaneity of approach worked both for and against Hughes. Many of his poems, written in hasty response to some event reported in yesterday's newspaper, for example, have badly dated. The spontaneity that resulted in his best poetry came from the depths of his own experiences as a black man in America, though these personal experiences often were disguised as archetypal ones.

The tension between his awareness of growing up black and his acceptance of the "dream" of America, however tenuously defined, provided the dynamic for his poetry. From an early age, Hughes developed the distinction between the social versus the physical implications of black identity in America: "You see, unfortunately, I am not black. There are lots of different kinds of blood in our family. But here in the United States, the work 'Negro' is used to mean anyone who has *any* Negro blood at all in his veins. In Africa, the word is more pure. It means *all* Negro, therefore *black*." During a trip to Africa as a merchant seaman in 1922, he discovered that the Africans who "looked at me . . . would not believe I was a Negro." The semantic confusion was of American origin. Whatever the semantic distinctions, Hughes desired to be accepted as Negro by the Africans, and was disappointed with their reaction to him.

Hughes's middle American background (he grew up in Lawrence, Kansas) sheltered him from some of the more blatant forms of racial prejudice toward Negroes in other regions of the country. When he lived in Topeka, he attended a white school, his mother having successfully challenged the school board to have him admitted. Most of his teachers were pleasant, but there was one "who sometimes used to make remarks about my being colored. And after such remarks, occasionally the kids would grab stones and tin cans out of the alley and chase me home." For a while he lived with his maternal grandmother, from whom he heard "beautiful stories about people who wanted to make the Negroes free, and how her father had apprenticed to him many slaves . . . so that they could work out their freedom. . . . Through my grandmother's stories always life moved, moved heroically toward an end. . . . Something about my grandmother's stories . . . taught me the uselessness of crying about anything." Hughes's poem "Aunt Sue's Stories," published in *The Crisis* in July of 1921, furnishes an example of how Hughes transformed such memories into poetry. His childhood was not a happy one in Lawrence, as he related in his autobiography, and he turned to books for solace. Parallels between his childhood experiences and later poems abound. Many of his poems focused on unhappy or wrongly treated children, for whom the American dream had no relevance. This empathy with wronged children had its origins in Hughes's own unhappiness as a child.

—Raymond Smith, "Langston Hughes: Evolution of the Poetic Persona" in *The Harlem Renaissance Re-examined*, ed. Victor A. Kramer (New York: AMS Press, 1987).

Martha Cobb on the Black Artist's Expression of African Themes

[Martha Cobb teaches Spanish at Howard University. She is the author of *Harlem, Haiti, and Havana: A Study of Langston Hughes, Jacques Roumain, and Nicholás Guillén* (1979). She has published widely on the black writers of the Caribbean.]

For black writers the imaginative expression of the African theme has had several dimensions. Among them have been the rejection of European cultural values and lament for a land that slavery has robbed blacks of, thematic concepts also found in the poetry of Jacques Roumain and Nicolas Guillen. In a poem he called "Black Seed" Hughes describes "World-wide dusk / Of dear dark faces / Driven before an alien wind / Scattered like seed . . . / In another's garden." He underscores the violence of the diaspora in subsequent lines—"Cut by the shears / Of the white-faced gardeners / —Tell them to leave you alone!"

Jacques Roumain, in his poetic description of "the long road to Guinée" employs similar imagery to emphasize the sense of loss, confrontation with an alien society, and the need to reject that society's imposition. Additionally, an "elegy" by Nicolás Guillén alludes with bitterness to the separation of black people from their ancestral home, pointedly describing the cruelty of the slave trade: "Along the sea roads / with the jasmine and the bull, / and with grain and iron / came the black man, to dig out the gold; / weeping in his exile / along the sea road."

To call the black point of view romantic in its nostalgia for a mythologized Africa, or unrealistic in its opposition to a culture that dominated it, is not to assess fully the obliquity of the perspective from which black poets could not escape as they looked out from within racial experiences onto a world that rejected their race. The poetry of alienation, lament, exile, and bitter memories which expresses a mythic image of Africa is part of a larger pattern which presents the black man as victim, outcast, and to a great extent scapegoat of Western civilization. Poetry on the subject of the slave trade embodies a racial memory which sings bitterly of blacks building a civilization whose benefits they do not share. Africa therefore becomes the *locus amoenus* where the victim/scapegoat becomes ideally reinstated as human being. This perception points to a major cleavage from the popular sentimental point of view, shared by most whites and some blacks, which sees the black as embodiment of either primitive innocence in its natural state, or of primitive— sometimes called "exotic"—passions whose jazz would release the industrialized West from the confinements of its inhibitions or from the madness of its wars. It was against this use of blacks as playthings and puppets that Guillén warned in "Pequeña oda a un negro boxeador" ("Small Ode to a Black Boxer") and that two other writers of Afro-Cuban poetry, Regino Pedroso and Marcelino Arozarena, denounced in "Hermano negro" ("Black Brother") and "Evohé" respectively.

In the first volume of his autobiography Hughes attacks the romantic view of the Negro as he describes the parting between himself and a wealthy patroness:

She wanted me to be primitive and know and feel the intuitions of the primitive. But, unfortunately, I did not feel the rhythms of the primitive surging through me, and so I could not live and write as though I did. I was only an American Negro—who had loved the surface of Africa—but I was not Africa. I was Chicago and Kansas City and Broadway and Harlem. And I was not what she wanted me to be.

—Martha Cobb, *Harlem, Haiti, and Havana: A Study of Langston Hughes, Jacques Roumain, and Nicholás Guillén* (Washington, D.C.: Three Continents Press, 1979).

Susan Blake on Hughes's "Simple" Stories

[Susan Blake is associate professor of English at Lafayette College and writes widely on black literature.]

In creating the Simple stories, Hughes has done the same thing with the black folk tradition that his character does with black history— made it live and work in the present. It is easily recognized that Hughes has a relationship to the folk tradition. He wrote poetry in vernacular language and blues form. He edited *The Book of Negro Humor* and, with Arna Bontemps, *The Book of Negro Folklore*, which includes several of his own poems and Simple stories as literature "in the folk manner." Simple himself has been called a "folk character" on the basis of half a dozen different definitions of the term: sociological average, composite of Southern folk types, epic hero, ordinary man, wise fool, blues artist. But Simple is more than vaguely "folk," and Hughes's relationship to the folk tradition is direct and dynamic. Simple is the migrant descendant of John, the militant slave of black folklore, and the fictional editorials that Hughes wrote for the *Chicago Defender* from 1943 to 1966 function as real folktales in the political story-telling tradition of the John-and-Old-Marster cycle. Not only do they follow the pattern of the John tales in characterization and conflict, not only do they include traditional motifs, they also recreate on the editorial page of a newspaper the dramatic relationship between storyteller and audience that characterizes an oral storytelling situation.

The principal difference between folk and self-conscious literature is the relationship between the work and the audience. Generally speaking, self-conscious literature, usually written, isolates the experience of individuals; is addressed to individuals, who may or may not share either personal or social experience with either the author or the characters; and is experienced by the individual as an individual. Folk literature, usually oral, isolates the experience of a socially defined group; is addressed to all members of the group; and is experienced by a group, even if it consists of only two members, as a group. The self-conscious artist tells a story to suit himself, and the audience takes it or leaves it. The folk storyteller chooses and adapts a traditional text according to the occasion and the audience. The folk audience, therefore, participates in the storytelling and, in a sense, is also part of the story told. The story is told by, to, and for the people it is about; it is part of their lives as they are part of it. The Simple stories close the gap between story and audience created by the medium of print in several ways. They, too, adapt traditional materials from black folklore, the Bible, U.S. history, and popular culture. They, too, are occasional, as they deal with current events and social conditions. Their consistent subject, race, is the one experience that unites and defines the folk group to which they are addressed. Their principal character is an avid reader of the very publication in which the audience encounters him. Their story-within-a-story structure creates a dialogue between characters and audience. And their purpose is to function in the social conflict in which both characters and audience are engaged.

—Susan L. Blake, "Old John in Harlem: The Urban Folktales of Langston Hughes," in *Black American Literature Forum* 25 (1991).

Arnold Rampersad on the Retrospective View of Hughes's Work

[Arnold Rampersad is director of the Program in Afro-American Studies and Woodrow Wilson Professor of Literature at Princeton University. He is the author of *The Art and Imagination of W. E. B. Du Bois*, as well as the definitive biography of Langston Hughes, *The Life of Langston Hughes*.]

At some point in his development, however, something happened to Hughes that was as mysterious and as wonderful, in its own way, as the miracle that overtook John Keats after the watchful night spent with his friend Charles Cowden Clarke and a copy of Chapman's translation. With "The Negro Speaks of Rivers" the creativity in Langston Hughes, hitherto essentially unexpressed, suddenly created itself.

In writing thus about Hughes, are we taking him too seriously? With a few exceptions, literary critics have resisted offering even a modestly complicated theory concerning his creativity. His relentless affability and charm, his deep, open love of the black masses, his devotion to their folk forms, and his insistence on writing poetry that they could understand, all have contributed to the notion that Langston Hughes was intellectually and emotionally shallow. One wonders, then, at the source of the creative energy that drove him from 1921 to 1967 to write so many poems, novels, short stories, plays, operas, popular histories, children's books, and assorted other work. As a poet, Hughes virtually reinvented Afro-American poetry with his pioneering use of the blues and other folk forms; as Howard Mumford Jones marveled in a 1927 review, Hughes added the verse form of the blues to poetry in English (a form that continues to attract the best black poets, including Michael Harper, Sherley Anne Williams, and Raymond Patterson). One wonders, too, in his aspect as a poet, why this apparently happy, apparently shallow man defined his creativity in terms of unhappiness. "I felt bad for the next three or four years," he would write in *The Big Sea* about the period beginning more or less with the publication of "The Negro Speaks of Rivers," "and those were the years when I wrote most of my poetry. (For my best poems were all written when I felt the worst. When I was happy, I didn't write anything.)"

Hughes actively promoted the image of geniality to which I have alluded. Wanting and needing to be loved, he scrubbed and polished his personality until there was no abrasive side, no jagged edge that might wound another human being. Publicly and privately, his manner belied the commonly held belief that creativity and madness are allied, that neuroses and a degree of malevolence are the fair price of art. His autobiographies, *The Big Sea* (1940) and *I Wonder as I Wander* (1956), made no enemies; to many readers, Hughes's mastery of that form consists in his ability to cross its chill deep by paddling nonchalantly on its surface. And yet in two places, no doubt deliberately, Hughes allows the reader a glimpse of inner turmoil. Both appear in the earlier book, *The Big Sea*. Both involve personal and emotional conflicts so intense that they led to physical illness. Because of their extreme rarity, as well as their strategic location in the context of his creativity, these passages deserve close scrutiny if we hope to glimpse the roots of Hughes's originality as a poet.

— Arnold Rampersad, "The Origins of Poetry in Langston Hughes," in *The Southern Review* 21 (1985).

MARYEMMA GRAHAM ON THE RELATIONSHIP BETWEEN THE ARTISTIC AND THE POLITICAL

[Maryemma Graham is associate professor of English and Afro-American Studies at Northeastern University. She is the author of *The Afro-American Novel* and editor of *How I Wrote Jubilee and Other Essays on Life and Literature* and *Complete Poems of Francis E. W. Harper.*]

As an independent radical, Hughes's thinking about literature and society did not constitute a formal ideology. He rejected the view that the writer's world view could be prescribed by the Communist Party during the 1930s. On a number of occasions Hughes was asked why he had not joined the party. His response to Arthur Koestler, whom he met in his travels in Soviet Russia, was typical:

> I told him that what I had heard concerning the party indicated that it was based on strict discipline and the acceptance of directives that I, as a writer, did not wish to accept. I did not believe political directive could be successfully applied to creative writing. They might well apply to the preparation of tracts and pamphlets, yes, but not to poetry or fiction, which to be valid, I felt, had to express as truthfully as possible the individual emotions and reactions of the writer, rather than mass directives issued to achieve practical and often temporary political objectives.

Hughes's rejection of the Communist Party was not a rejection of the view that the struggle for socialism was a struggle for a better society. The determination of the specific relation between politics and literature which the majority of American proletarian writers accepted in the form of commandments, borrowed from the Soviet example, did not take into consideration the particularities of the Black American experience; this fact Hughes realized. Thus, Hughes could actively support the Socialist/Communist philosophy but would work out his own particular approach to a socialized art. His point of departure was the black experience.

It is clear that Hughes consistently appealed for a black national expression in literature. For him, the relationship between the artistic and the political had to be defined in terms of the artist's relationship to black life. The work of the artist assumes political significance as the artist perceives his importance in establishing the priorities of black life. Hughes himself was extraordinarily perceptive in this regard. By reaching into the rich empirical evidence of the life and culture of black people, he was continuously updating an authentic national expression, that is, the musical forms, vernacular language, and other peculiarly oral forms of expression, and the social (secular and religious) customs associated with the black working class, partly rural but increasingly urban. It was Langston Hughes, more than any other black artist during the 1930s, who realized the political implications of the cultural manifestations of the national oppression of the black masses. He proposed cultural nationalism—the overt physical, emotional, and psychological manifestations of the struggle of black people. It was, however, the collective and, by implication, communal nature of the black experience, embodied in the wealth of folkloric material, that made cultural nationalism, not alien to, but the base upon which any consciousness of economic exploitation within the class structure of the American capitalist society would have to depend. Moreover, Hughes realized that the majority of black people saw themselves as an element of the American population who were defined racially; their history and culture attested to this fact. It was, however, this particular fact that made the general functions of capitalist society more operational. Hughes's works are a real indication of the necessity and the possibility of using the particular facts of the experience of black people to reach a broader understanding of the general nature of society.

—Maryemma Graham, "The Practice of a Social Art," in *Langston Hughes: Critical Perspectives Past and Present*, ed. Henry Louis Gates Jr. and K. A. Appiah (New York: Amistad Press, 1993). ⑨

Thematic Analysis of
"Song for a Dark Girl"

In the 1940s, as the era of civil rights and integration approached, a new generation of young black writers and artists—Richard Wright, Gwendolyn Brooks, Melvin Tolson, Robert Hayden, Ralph Ellison, and James Baldwin, to name a few—emerged to champion the struggle against white oppression. Hughes, by this time a literary legend, felt a strained, problematic relationship with this new generation. Hughes considered himself a writer and advocate of his people; his love for his people did not, however, translate into a desire to go into battle for them. His fear of confrontation, ideological or otherwise, and his vaguely antiassimilationist sensibilities brought strong criticism from this new set of black artists: His work lacked intellectual rigor, and he lacked commitment to the growing conflict between the races.

Ralph Ellison reviewed *The Big Sea*, Hughes's first autobiography, in 1940, calling it a "chit-chat book," unworthy of a man of Hughes's experience and power. Hughes responded, "If I wrote the book you wanted me to write, people wouldn't buy it, and I would have to take a job" (Ralph Ellison, in Arnold Rampersad, *The Life of Langston Hughes, 1902–1967*, 2 vols. [New York: Oxford University Press 1986–88], p. 202). This appalled Ellison, who considered himself an artist and crusader for black equality and incapable of such compromise.

Hughes was not insensitive to the brute force of American racism, as he shows in "Song for a Dark Girl," but this is not what he would demarcate as his particular literary terrain. The Harlem Renaissance, from which he had emerged as an artist, allowed him full freedom to focus on the black experience in itself and to leave the conflict between the races largely alone. With integration becoming reality, however, Hughes struggled to hold on to his original position.

Hughes admired these young black crusaders but disapproved of the distance they deliberately placed between themselves and the black masses they championed. Hughes once quipped, after a brief meeting with Ellison, that he "looked fat, fine, and worried (about the Hungarians and such) as usual" (Rampersad, *The Life of Langston Hughes*, p. 296). Hughes saw a self-conscious intellectualism and hauteur in Ellison that from his earliest days he always despised, especially when it replaced human warmth and a sense of shared values.

"Song for a Dark Girl" is one of the rare instances in which Hughes uses racial brutality as a theme. Even here, however, the violence is secondary to the girl's grief and her reproach of God. Set in the South, the verse form recalls Dixieland rhythms, and the effect is bitter irony. Hughes's experiences in the Deep South were concentrated in the two summers he spent touring with Zora Neale Hurston in the 1920s; during that time he saw a hardened prejudice that made Northern racism pale by comparison. Lynchings, in particular, were almost strictly Southern incidents, and Christian doctrine was frequently the only justification. The richness of Southern black folk tradition captivated Hughes and became the very basis of his art, but the barbarity of the setting indelibly impressed itself on his mind and his work. Hughes's poem "The South" illustrates his complicated feelings for the South, teeming with racial hatred and black folklore:

> The lazy, laughing South
> With blood on its mouth.
> The sunny-faced South,
>   Beast-strong,
>   Idiot-brained.
> The child-minded South
> Scratching in the dead fire's ashes
> For a Negro's bones.
>   Cotton and the moon,
>   Warmth, earth, warmth
>   The sky, the sun, the stars,
>   The magnolia-scented South.
> Beautiful, like a woman,
> Seductive as a dark-eyed whore,
>   Passionate, cruel,
>   Honey-lipped, syphilitic—
>   That is the South.
> And I, who am black, would love her
> But she spits in my face.
> And I, who am black,
> Would give her many rare gifts
> But she turns her back upon me.
>   So now I seek the North—
>   The cold-faced North,

> For she, they say,
> Is a kinder mistress,
> And in her house my children
> May escape the spell of the South.

When the girl in "Song for a Dark Girl" asks what the use of praying is, Hughes reveals his lifelong suspicion of religion. As a child in Kansas, Hughes went to church and was asked by the preacher to "receive Jesus." The aftermath of this experience was recorded in his first autobiography, *The Big Sea*: "That night, for the last time in my life but one ... I cried. ... I couldn't bear to tell her [my aunt] that I ... hadn't seen Jesus, and that now I didn't believe there was a Jesus any more" (Gates and Appiah, *Langston Hughes*, p. 173). This anti-religious stance did not diminish, however, his attraction to gospel music, Southern spiritualism, and the idea of Christ—particularly the notion of Christ as one of the masses, as in the poem "Ma Lord":

> Ma Lord ain't no stuck-up man,
> Ma Lord he ain't proud.
> When he goes a-walkin'
> He gives me his hand.
> "You ma friend," he 'lowed.

And in one of Hughes's most provocative poems, "Christ in Alabama," Hughes conflates the lynched black man with Jesus on the cross.

Hughes refused to blur his focus on the day-to-day lives and traditions of his people. His acute awareness of history and discrimination percolated through his poetry delicately, but rarely dominated his work. Arnold Rampersad explains Hughes's position within the Afro-American literary tradition:

> His attitude spoke, paradoxically, for the depth of his identification with the race, which freed him not only to understand that the profession of writing was distinct from its "subject," but also to see his race in a rounded humane way, rather than mainly as a deformed product of white racism. (*The Life of Langston Hughes*, vol. 2, p. 296)

Hughes played a pivotal role in placing black literature in the American canon and preserving the uniqueness of the black folk tradition but he was not a political poet. He protested the restriction of expression and the exclusion of cultures, and in effect, became a poet of change and progress.

"Song for a Dark Girl" is the first-person narrative of a Southern girl tortured by the image of her dead lover: "Love is a naked shadow / on a gnarled and naked tree." The girl asks "the white Lord Jesus / What was the use of prayer." She projects no hope, and she condemns no one. Hughes does not sermonize: He presents an uncomplicated picture of a despairing girl as she wonders why her God, even being white, has not come to her aid. Hughes dispenses with commentary, not allowing it to diminish the power of the image.

When literatures of protest were proliferating, Hughes stood his own ground, still supporting the efforts of the younger black writers. They did not always respect him for it, however. James Baldwin reviewed Hughes's *Selected Poems* in 1959 harshly, which wounded Hughes deeply: "I am amazed all over again by his genuine gifts— and depressed that he has done so little with them" (Rampersad, *The Life of Langston Hughes*, p. 295). Baldwin's heightened social consciousness and position at the front of the new black movement clouded his view of the past, of those who had paved the road he himself tread. Many years later, Baldwin would think back with some distress on this review: "I hadn't really read the book, to tell the truth. I wrote the review without fully understanding what I was doing and saying." (Rampersad, *The Life of Langston Hughes*, p. 299)

In an interview with the writer Clayton Riley, Baldwin added:

> I suppose it's not too much to say that reading Langston made me understand something about my father's rages, and my mother's seeming passivity, and the people on the streets, the people in the church, the deacons, sisters and brothers. When I read Langston, it was like I was reading a book and looking up and what was on the page was in a sense right before my eyes. But he helped me see it, you know. He helped me to locate myself in it." (Rampersad, *The Life of Langston Hughes*, p. 299) ❀

Critical Views on
"Song for a Dark Girl"

JAMES A. EMANUEL ON HUGHES'S DEPICTION OF RACIAL
VIOLENCE

[James A. Emanuel is the author of *Black Man Abroad: The
Toulouse Poems, Panther Man, Langston Hughes,* and the
editor of *Dark Symphony: Negro Literature in America.*]

In other poems and stories, the viciousness of racial violence, sometimes fatal, is not transformed by religious emphasis but by style.
"Southern Mammy Sings" (*Poetry,* May 1941) begins humorously
("Miss Gardner's in her garden. / Miss Yardman's in her yard."),
modulates the harshness of its meaning through the use of dialect,
then ends:

> Last week they lynched a colored boy.
> They hung him to a tree.
> That colored boy ain't said a thing
> But we all should be free.
>   Yes, ma'am!
> We all should be free.
>
> Not meanin' to be sassy
> And not meanin' to be smart—
> But sometimes I think that white folks
> Just ain't go no heart.
>   No. ma'am!
> Just ain't got no heart.

These words are a subtle play upon Southern custom and history.
The Negro "mammy," mother to Negro youth and motherly nurse to
whites who will likely grow up to abuse them, sings (a lovely sign of
her contentment) about her travail. Her superficial apology for
being so "sassy" as to pass judgment upon the murderous bent of
whites accentuates the heroic silence of the boy who died like the
victim in Vernon Loggins's story "Neber Said a Mumblin Word."

It may be surprising that only about a score of the hundreds of
poems written by Hughes strongly develop this theme of violence.
Yet several of these are memorable. His "Roland Hayes Beaten,"

imbued with the slow fire of modern Negro spirit, supplied the motto and refrain for the pamphlet printed by the National Association for the Advancement of Colored People (February 1962), *The Day They Changed Their Minds*, to commemorate the sit-in demonstrations that have brought historic upheaval to the South. The poem is brief:

> Negroes,
> Sweet and docile,
> Meek, humble, and kind:
> Beware the day
> They change their minds!
>
> Wind
> In the cotton fields,
> Gentle breeze:
> Beware the hour
> It uproots trees!

The *Negro Handbook* for 1944 reads: "July 11 [1942]—Roland Hayes, internationally famous tenor, was beaten by three white policemen in Rome, Ga., where he lived with his family, following a brief argument that his wife had with a shoe store clerk." In the poem, Hughes elevates the gentle artist's ordeal into a tense warning. The repetition of "beware," the contrast between "day" and "hour," the analogy of the wind that brings both static sweetness and rushing holocaust—all are restrained prophecy. The physically precarious balance in the single-word lines carries much of the meaning. The poet's steadying irony insured artistic quality.

> —James A. Emanuel, *Langston Hughes* (New York: Twayne Publishers, Inc., 1967).

R. BAXTER MILLER ON HUGHES'S PRESENTATION OF THE MATRIARCHAL ARCHETYPE

[R. Baxter Miller is professor of English and director of the Black Literature Program at the University of Tennessee, Knoxville. He is the author of *Langston Hughes and Gwen-*

dolyn Brooks: A Reference Guide and *For a Moment I Wondered: The Literary Imagination of Langston Hughes* (1986).]

Langston Hughes's "Mother to Son" and "Negro Mother," however, combine Christian myth and folk experience. In them the poet deals with a problem of religious belief and thus becomes one of several American poets to do so. Our literary artists have believed (or disbelieved) in God, the American Dream, the Power of Transcendence, or the American Myth. Edward Taylor and William Cullen Bryant believed in God. Emerson believed in transcendence, and his contemporary, Whitman, believed in himself. Whitman also had faith in a poetic power that could rejuvenate the world or that could at least reinvigorate the world through enthusiastic perception. Wallace Stevens, humanistic like Whitman, believed more in man than in External Divinity. To Stevens, indeed, man *was* divinity, since divinity must "live within herself." Closer still to our time, T. S. Eliot has restored to our poetry a sense of the Externally Divine. Even more recently, Allen Ginsberg has laughed at American myth by saying that he is putting his "queer shoulder" to the country's wheel.

But no American poet, I think, combines myth and pragmatism better than Hughes does in poems presenting matriarchal archetypes. Indeed, Hughes himself will never do so again. In the 1950s he will turn his attention more to prose than to poetry. Returning to the writing of verse in the sixties, he will miss his once lyrical gift. Slowly but surely social injustice whittles away hopeful vision.

Fortunately Hughes left to posterity his earlier image of the black woman who can tell stories about her yesterdays. She sometimes becomes a means of discoursing on youth, which is gone forever, while at other times, unable to transcend adversity, she becomes a personified portrait of trouble, occasionally sublimated into art. We must sometimes laugh at her confrontation with mortality, at her attempts to transcend adversity, if only to avoid crying at her weariness, at the bitterness surrounding the racial quest. But ultimately we must admire her incarnate heroic determination, the Black Spirit.

—R. Baxter Miller, " 'No Crystal Stair': Unity, Archetype and Symbol in Langston Hughes's Poems on Women," in *Negro American Literature Forum* 9 (1975).

Onwuchekwa Jemie on Hughes's Religious Poems and Themes

[Onwuchekwa Jemie is the author of *Langston Hughes: An Introduction to the Poetry* (1973).]

In the poem "Scottsboro" the youths are identified with Jesus Christ, John Brown, Nat Turner, Gandhi, and other martyrs. These men are not dead, Hughes declares, they are immortal; and "Is it much to die when immortal feet / March with you down Time's street . . . ?" In "Christ in Alabama" Jesus is pictured as a lynched black man:

> Christ is a nigger,
> Beaten and black:
> Oh, bare your back!
>
> Mary is His mother;
> Mammy of the South,
> Silence your mouth.
>
> God is His father:
> White Master above
> Grant Him your love.
>
> Most holy bastard
> Of the bleeding mouth,
> Nigger Christ
> On the cross
> Of the South.

"Christ is a nigger" in two senses: in the historical sense as a brown-skinned Jew like other Jews of his day, with a brown-skinned mother—both later adopted into the white West and given a lily-white heavenly father; and in the symbolic sense of Jesus as an alien presence, preaching an exacting spirituality, a foreign religion as it were, much as the black man, with his different color and culture, is an alien presence in the South. Each is a scapegoat sacrificed for the society's sins. In particular, the white skin of lust has created a mongrel mulatto race ("most holy bastard") with black slave mothers ("Mammy of the South") and white slavemaster fathers ("White Master above"). And, once created, this race is cast out, disinherited, crucified.

A later poem, "Bible Belt," amplifies and illuminates "Christ in Alabama":

> It would be too bad if Jesus
> Were to come back black.
> There are so many churches
> Where he could not pray
> In the U.S.A.,
> Where entrance to Negroes,
> No matter how sanctified,
> Is denied,
> Where race, not religion,
> Is glorified.
> But say it—
> *You* may be
> Crucified.

If they remembered Jesus in his historical identity ("nigger"), the white people of the United States would not so readily call themselves Christians. Hughes recalls an occasion when students at the University of North Carolina at Chapel Hill printed "Christ in Alabama" on the front page of their newspaper on the day he was scheduled to speak at the university. Some of the townspeople, including the sheriff, suggested that the poet be run out of town: "It's bad enough to call Christ a bastard. But when he calls him a nigger, he's gone too far!"

The cryptic simplicity of "Christ in Alabama" exhibits Hughes at his best. Profound insight is carelessly draped in the most facile diction and form, the most commonplace images. There is no decoration or pedantry. The poem is so stark it could almost have been written by a child. It reminds one of classic African sculpture, with its bold lined and geometric precision. The poem evokes the feeling that great art so often evokes: that it could not have been done any other way. It commands both accessibility and depth. Hughes is a master at clothing the complex and profound in simple garb; and perhaps it is this more than any other quality that marks him as a great poet.

—Onwuchekwa Jemie, *Langston Hughes: An Introduction to the Poetry* (New York: Columbia University Press, 1976).

[Arnold Rampersad is director of the Program in Afro-
American Studies and Woodrow Wilson Professor of Litera-
ture at Princeton University. He is the author of *The Art and
Imagination of W. E. B. Du Bois*, as well as the definitive
biography of Langston Hughes, *The Life of Langston
Hughes*.]

For his first few years as a poet, even as he grew technically profi-
cient, Hughes had no idea what to do with a form he had heard first
as a child in Lawrence, Kansas, and in Kansas City, Missouri. Even
then he had responded emotionally, as he would assert, to the deep,
piercing sadness of the music; later, no doubt, he began to marvel at
its curious, accompanying impulse toward laughter. But how was he
to effect a link between his learned standards of formal poetry and
songs created by the artist among the masses? This question mas-
querades as one simply of technique; however, it concerns not only
the realities of political power—the social powerlessness of blacks
translated into the declassification of their art—but the ability of the
individual to attain a sufficiently deep identification with his people
and their modes of utterance so that, on an individual initiative, he
is able to affect a dignified fusion of learned poetic values with those
of the despised masses.

When Hughes opened his greatest essay, "The Negro Artist and
the Racial Mountain" (1926) by equating the desire of a certain
young black poet to be seen as nothing but a poet with the desire to
be white, he was (perhaps reductively) stating his understanding of
the most complex problem facing the young black writer. Hughes
and, no doubt, some other young black writers had no literal desire
to be white. Nevertheless, the domination of white poetic standards
through the many unquestionably alluring volumes of white verse,
backed ultimately by the domination of white culture, effectively
made their dilemma forbiddingly close to that of a racial death-wish
described by Hughes at the start of the essay. Because his will to
solve this conundrum was so strong, however, Langston Hughes progressed where others stagnated. But he progressed only in stages.

Not long after "The Negro Speaks of Rivers," Hughes began to
offer, as poetry, the barely mediated recording of the sounds and

sights of black life, notably in religion. One poem, "Prayer Meeting" (1922–1923), may stand here as an example.

> Glory! Hallelujah!
> The dawn's a-comin'!
> Glory! Hallelujah!
> The dawn's a-comin'!
> A black old woman croons
> In the amen-corner of the
> Ebecaneezer Baptist Church—
> A black old woman croons—
> The dawn's a-comin'!

In his willingness to stand back and record, with minimal intervention, aspects of the drama of black religion (and, later, of music and dance), Hughes clearly showed that he had begun to see his own learned poetic art, even with his individual talent, as inferior to that of "ordinary" blacks—inferior, for example, to an old black woman in the amen corner who cries to Jesus, "Glory! Hallelujah!" At the heart of his sense of inferiority—which empowered rather than debilitated Hughes—was the knowledge that he (and other wouldbe poets) stood to a great extent outside the culture he worshiped. Perhaps Hughes stood at a greater distance from the masses than did most other black poets. Raised in relative isolation and with a haunting sense of parental abandonment, he stood outside because much of his life had been spent away from consistent involvement with the very people whose affection and regard he craved.

—Arnold Rampersad, "Langston Hughes's *Fine Clothes to the Jew*," in *Callaloo* 9 (1986).

LESLIE CATHERINE SANDERS ON HUGHES'S EXPLORATION OF RELIGIOSITY

[Leslie Catherine Sanders is associate professor of Humanities and English and coordinator of writing programs at Atkinson College, York University, Ontario. Her book *The Development of Black Theater in America* was published by Louisiana State University Press in 1988.]

Secular to the bone, as biographer Arnold Rampersad characterized him, Langston Hughes was notoriously reticent on matters of religion: "In an envelope marked: / Personal / God addressed me a letter. / In an envelope marked: / Personal / I have given my answer," he wrote enigmatically in 1935, in response to renewed attacks over his infamous 1932 poem "Good-bye Christ." As a rule, Hughes stayed away from religious topics and themes, although he loved and respected the distinctive manifestations of black religious practice, and occasionally did draw on its forms and imagery. An early and notable poetic example is the "Glory! Hallelujah!" sequence in *Fine Clothes to the Jew* (1927), his second volume of poetry. Hughes's most extended use of religious material occurs in his plays, where his impulse to record the drama of black music and black religion found appropriate form.

Religious material first appears in Hughes's work for the theatre in *Don't You Want to Be Free?*, a "music-drama" written in 1937 expressly for his Harlem Suitcase Theater. In this chronicle of the black experience, Hughes uses spirituals to voice the sufferings of the slaves; for later sequences, he uses his own poetry. Religious sentiments, in this play, are positioned historically; the play moves its audience toward a secularly defined and self-reliant revolt, rather than a divinely inspired strength to endure.

Hughes's next dramatic exploration of religious material extends, and even corrects, this earlier effort. Arnold Rampersad suggests that Hughes's residence at the home of the devout Noel Sullivan encouraged "stirrings of religion in him," but Hughes may as well have been inspired by his tentative dramatic exploration, in the earlier work, of religious music as an articulation of black striving. Also written for a theatre he founded, the Skyloft Players, *The Sun Do Move* (1942) is the story of a slave named Rock, and his efforts to bring his family to freedom. In the original sermon from which the play takes its name, the preacher, John Jasper of Virginia, pitted his faith in God and the Biblical word, particularly Joshua 10:13, against science and "new discoveries" about the stationary Sun and revolving Earth. In Hughes's play, only Rock's faith and imagination make his escape to freedom possible because, empirically, freedom does not exist. The reality of enslavement has robbed his fellow slaves of the ability to seek freedom, even to know in what direction it might lie. *The Sun Do Move*, which begins in Africa and ends as Rock goes off to war with the Union army, exploits both the religious and secular meanings of the spirituals, for whether they are sung as an individual's or a group's response to events, or simply as a bridge between scenes, they continually draw upon both their levels of meaning—as songs of faith and as maps of the route to freedom. *The Sun Do Move* is, in part, a play about the meaning of the spirituals, and so not only a "music-play," as Hughes called it, but also a drama about the music itself.

There were few precedents for Hughes's foray into music plays about black music. Notably, his precursor was Hall Johnson's *Run Little Chillun*, first produced on Broadway in 1933, which Johnson described to Doris Abramson as "what's behind the spirituals." But Johnson's play, a clear response to *The Green Pastures*, for which Hall Johnson's choir provided the music, focused on the African roots of black Christianity in its portrait of the conflict between the Hope Baptist Church and the pantheistic New Day Pilgrims, not on the music itself.

In bringing the black church, and black religious music, to the stage, Hughes was, in his characteristic fashion, not only breaking new ground but also challenging white conventional depictions of black folk life. For example, presented frivolously in *The Prayer Meeting* and seriously in *Your Fiery Furnace*, both by the white playwright Paul Green, black religion and church service assume the shape of set responses, displays of characteristic behavior rather than serious explorations of the meaning of black belief. Just as Hall Johnson's *Run Little Chillun* constituted a rebuke to *The Green Pastures*, Hughes undertook first to explore and then to reappropriate the dramatic presentation of black religion and its music.

—Leslie Catherine Sanders, "'I've wrestled with them all my life': Langston Hughes's *Tambourines to Glory*," in *Black American Literature Forum* 25 (1991).

STEVEN TRACY ON HUGHES'S APPROPRIATION OF SPIRITUALS AND GOSPEL MUSIC

[Stephen Tracy lives and works in Cincinnati. He is the author of *Langston Hughes and the Blues* and *Going to Cincinnati: A History of the Blues in the Queen City.*]

It is clear that Hughes did not exalt spirituals and gospel music based on any fervent belief in Christianity. The "Salvation" chapter in *The Big Sea* outlines his traumatic (non-) conversion experience that left him doubting the existence of a Jesus who had not come to help him; and his poem "Mystery" describes the feelings of an uninitiated thirteen-year-old, isolated by her confused uncertainty, yoking "The mystery / and the darkness / and the song / and me." In "To Negro Writers" he called on his African American colleagues to "expose the sick-sweet smile of organized religion . . . and the half-voodoo, half-clown face of revivalism, dulling the mind with the clap of its empty hands." His "first experience with censorship" he recounted in "My Adventures as a Social Poet," reporting how a preacher directed him not to read any more blues in his pulpit. Years later in a Simple story, "Gospel Singers," Simple compares churches to movie theaters, preachers to movie stars, and church services to shows during which gospel singers are "working in the vineyards of the Lord and digging in his gold mines," joking that when you hear gospel singers "crying 'I Cannot Bear My Burden Alone,' what they really mean is, 'Help me get my cross to my Cadillac.'" Significantly, though, Simple did not mind paying to hear the gospel singers— paying twice, even—because he felt that "the music that these people put down can't be beat" For Simple, as for Hughes, it was not the meaning of the words so much as the wording of the means that carried him away. What Hughes said about the blues in "Songs Called the Blues" applies to gospel music as well: "You don't have to understand the words to know the meaning of the blues, or to feel their sadness or to hope their hopes."

—Steven Tracy, *Langston Hughes: The Man, His Art, and His Continuing Influence* (New York/London: Garland Publishing, 1995).

Arnold Rampersad on Hughes's Break with Traditional Forms

[Arnold Rampersad is director of the Program in Afro-American Studies and Woodrow Wilson Professor of Literature at Princeton University. He is the author of *The Art and Imagination of W. E. B. Du Bois*, as well as the definitive biography of Langston Hughes, *The Life of Langston Hughes*.]

From the start of his publishing in the *Crisis* magazine, Hughes had shown his determination to experiment as a poet and not slavishly follow the tyranny of tight stanzaic forms and exact rhyme. He seemed to prefer, as had Walt Whitman and Carl Sandburg before him, to write verse that captured the realities of American speech, rather than "poetic diction," and with his ear especially attuned to the varieties of black American speech. This last aspect was a token of his emotional and esthetic involvement in black American culture, which he took as his prime source of inspiration. African Americans were "My people," as one of his early poems proclaims. His first book, *The Weary Blues*, combines these various elements: the common speech of ordinary people, jazz and blues music, and the traditional forms of poetry adapted to the African American and American subjects. The volume was unprecedented in American poetry in this blending of black and white rhythms and forms.

One cannot talk definitively about Langston Hughes the man, his work, and continuing influence without referring to his 1926 essay "The Negro Artist and the Racial Mountain," which was virtually a cultural manifesto for many of the younger writers of the Harlem Renaissance. In it, Hughes declared:

> We younger Negro artists . . . intend to express our individual dark–skinned selves without fear or shame. If white people are pleased we are glad. If they are not, it doesn't matter. We know we are beautiful. And ugly too. The tom-tom cries and the tom-tom laughs. If colored people are pleased we are glad. If they are not, their displeasure doesn't matter either. We build our temples for tomorrow, strong as we know how, and we stand on top of the mountain, free within ourselves.

In talking thus far about Hughes the man and his work I have not mentioned such major crises of his life as his break around 1930 with his major patron of the 1920s, Mrs. Charlotte Mason, or "God-mother," as she liked to be called; or with Zora Neale Hurston, another beneficiary of Mrs. Mason's largesse, a short time later. Nor have I mentioned Hughes's turn to the radical left in the wake of these episodes of disillusionment. From being a poet of blues and jazz he turned toward being a radical socialist poet, as in works such as "Good Morning Revolution" and "Goodbye Christ," as well as *Scottsboro Limited*, about the infamous Scottsboro case, and *Don't You Want to be Free?*, Hughes's radical play with the Harlem Suitcase Theater in 1938.

However, Hughes was not solely a radical poet during this time. In various plays, including *Mulatto* on Broadway in 1935 and other works staged by the Karamu Theater in Cleveland, Hughes empha-sized the ways of racism or wrote comedies of African American life. In any event, his radical socialist phase more or less ended around 1940, when he returned, as he himself mordantly put it, to "Negroes, Nature, and Love."

—Arnold Rampersad, *Langston Hughes: The Man, His Art, and His Continuing Influence* (New York/London: Garland Publishing, 1995).

Works by
Langston Hughes

Volumes of Poetry

The Weary Blues (1926)

Fine Clothes to the Jew (1927)

Dear Lovely Death (1931)

The Negro Mother and Other Dramatic Recitations (1931)

The Dream Keeper and Other Poems (1932)

Scottsboro Limited: Four Poems and a Play (1932)

A New Song (1938)

Shakespeare in Harlem (1942)

Jim Crow's Last Stand (1943)

Freedom's Plow (1943)

Lament for Dark Peoples and Other Poems (1944)

Fields of Wonder (1947)

One-Way Ticket (1949)

Montage of a Dream Deferred (1951)

Ask Your Mama: Twelve Moods for Jazz (1961)

The Panther and the Lash (1967)

Novels

Not Without Laughter (1930)

Tambourines to Glory (1958)

Short Story Collections

The Ways of White Folks (1934)

Simple Speaks His Mind (1950)

Laughing to Keep from Crying (1952)

Simple Takes a Wife (1953)

Simple Stakes a Claim (1957)

Something in Common and Other Stories (1963)

Simple's Uncle Sam (1965)

Autobiographies

The Big Sea (1940)

I Wonder as I Wander (1956)

Nonfiction

A Negro Looks at the Soviet Central Asia (1934)

The Book of Negro Folklore (with Arna Bontemps) (1958)

Fight for Freedom: The Story of the NAACP (with Milton Meltzer) (1962)

Black Magic: A Pictorial History of the African-American in the Performing Arts (1967)

For Young People

Popo and Fifina (with Arna Bontemps) (1932)

The Pasteboard Bandit (with Arna Bontemps) (1934)

The First Book of Negroes (with Arna Bontemps) (1952)

Famous American Negroes (1953)

The First Book of Rhythms (1954)

The First Book of the Caribbean (1954)

The First Book of Jazz (1955)

First Book of the West Indies (1956)

Famous Negro Heroes of America (1958)

First Book of Africa (1960)

The Sweet and Sour Animal Book (1994; posthumous)

Plays

Mule Bone (1930)

Mulatto (1935)

Little Ham (1935)

When Jack Hollers (1936)

Troubled Island (1936)

Emperor of Haiti (1936)

Front Porch (1937)

Joy to My Soul (1937)

Soul Gone Home (1937)

Little Eva's End (1938)
The Em-Fuehrer Jones (1938)
Don't You Want to Be Free (1938)
The Organizer (1939)
The Sun Do Move (1942)
Way Down South (screenplay) (1942)
For This We Fight (1943)
The Glory Around His Head (1953)
Esther (1957)
Simply Heavenly (1957)
The Ballad of the Brown King (1960)
Black Nativity (1961)
Gospel Glow (1962)
Tambourines to Glory (1963)
Jericho-Jim Crow (1963)
Soul Gone Home (1963)
The Prodigal Son (1965)

Other

Street Scene, lyrics for an opera by Kurt Weil (1948)

Poetry of the Negro, anthology compiled with Arna Bontemps (1949)
The Story of Jazz, album recorded (1954)
The Glory of Negro History, album recorded (1954)
Sweet Flypaper of Life, text for a book of photographs by Roy DeCarava (1955)
Selected Poems, poems compiled (1959)
An African Treasury: Articles, Essays, Stories, and Poems by Black Africans, anthology compiled (1960)
Poems from Black Africa, Ethiopia, and Other Countries, edited (1963)
New Negro Poets USA, anthology compiled (1964)
The Book of Negro Humor, edited (1966)
The Best Short Stories by Negro Writers, edited (1967)

Works about
Langston Hughes

Ako, Edward O. "Langston Hughes and the Negritude Movement: A Study in Literary Influence." *College Language Association Journal* 28 (1983–84): 46–56.

Appiah, K. A., and Henry Louis Gates, Jr., eds. *Langston Hughes: Critical Perspectives Past and Present.* New York: Amistad Press, 1993.

Barksdale, Richard K. *Langston Hughes: The Poet and His Critics.* Chicago: American Library Association, 1977.

Berry, Faith. *Langston Hughes: Before and Beyond Harlem.* Westport, Conn.: Lawrence Hill, 1983.

Beyer, William C. "A Certain Kind of Aesthete: Langston Hughes's Shakespeare in Harlem." In *A Humanist's Legacy: Essays in Honor of John Christian Bale,* edited by Dennis M. Jones. Decorah, Iowa: Luther College, 1990.

Blake, Susan L. "The American Dream and the Legacy of Revolution in the Poetry of Langston Hughes." *Black American Literature Forum* 14 (1980): 100–104.

Bogumil, Mary L., and Michael R. Moliao. "Pretext, Context, Subtext: Textual Power in the Writing of Langston Hughes, Richard Wright, and Martin Luther King, Jr." *College English* 52 (Nov. 1990): 800–12.

Brown, Lloyd W. "The Portrait of the Artist as a Black American in the Poetry of Langston Hughes." *Studies in Black Literature* 5, no. 1 (1974): 24–27.

Bruck, Peter. "Langston Hughes: 'The Blues I'm Playing' (1934)." In *The Black American Short Story in the 20th Century: A Collection of Critical Essays,* edited by Peter Bruck. Amsterdam: B. R. Gruner, 1977.

Bontemps, Arna. *The Harlem Renaissance Remembered.* New York: Dodd, Mead, 1972.

Clark, VeVe. "Restaging Langston Hughes's Scottsboro Limited: An Interview with Amiri Baraka." *Black Scholar* 10 (1979): 62–69.

Clarke, John Herrik. "The Neglected Dimensions of the Harlem Renaissance." *Black World* 20 (November 1970): 118–29.

Cobb, Martha K. "Concepts of Blackness in the Poetry of Nicholas Guillen, Jacques Romain, and Langston Hughes." *College Language Association Journal* 18 (1974–75): 262–72.

Cullen, Countee. "Poet on Poet." *Opportunity* 4 (March 1926): 73.

Davis, Arthur P. "The Harlem of Langston Hughes's Poetry." *Phylon* 13 (Winter 1952): 276–83.

———. "Langston Hughes." In *From the Dark Tower*. Washington, D.C.: Howard University Press, 1974.

———. "The Tragic Mulatto Theme in Six Works of Langston Hughes." *Phylon* 16 (Spring 1955): 195–204.

Dickinson, Donald C. *A Bio-Bibliography of Langston Hughes, 1902–1967*. Hamden, Conn.: Archon, 1967.

———. "Langston Hughes and the Brownie's Book." *Negro History Bulletin* 31 (December 1968): 8–10.

Dixon, Melvin. "Rivers Remembering Their Source: Comparative Studies in Black Literary History—Langston Hughes, Jacques Romain, and Negritude." In *Afro-American Literature: The Reconstruction of Instruction*, edited by Dexter Fisher and Robert B. Stepto. New York: Modern Language Association, 1979.

Emanuel, James A. *Langston Hughes*. New York: Twayne, 1967.

Fauset, Jesse. "Review of The Weary Blues." *Crisis* 34 (March 1926): 239.

Franke, Thomas L. "The Art of Verbal Performance: A Stylistic Analysis of Langston Hughes's 'Feet Live Their Own Life.'" *Language and Style: An International Journal* 19 (Fall 1986): 377–87.

Gates, Henry Louis, Jr. "The Hungry Icon: Langston Hughes Rides a Blue Note." *Village Voice Literary Supplement* (July 1989): 8–13.

———. "Why the 'Mule Bone' Debate Goes On." *New York Times, Arts and Leisure* (10 February 1991): 5, 8.

Gomes, E. "The Crackerbox Tradition and the Race Problem in Lowell's *The Bigelow Papers* and Hughes's *Sketches of Simple*." *College Language Association Journal* 27 (1983–84): 254–69.

Hansell, William H. "Black Music in the Poetry of Langston Hughes: Roots, Race, Release." *Obsidian* 4 (Winter 1978): 16–38.

Jackson, Blyden. "Claude McKay and Langston Hughes: The Harlem Renaissance and More." *Pembroke Magazine* 6 (1975): 43–48.

———. "From One 'New Negro' to Another." In *Black Poetry in America: Two Essays on Historical Interpretation*. Baton Rouge: Louisiana State University Press, 1974.

———. "Renaissance in the Twenties." In *The Twenties: Fiction, Poetry, Drama*, edited by Warren French. Deland, Fla.: Everett/Edwards, 1975.

———. "A Word about Simple." *College Language Association Journal* 11 (1967–68): 310–18.

Jemie, Onwuchekwa. *Langston Hughes: An Introduction to the Poetry*. New York: Columbia University Press, 1976.

Kent, George E. "Langston Hughes and the Afro-American Folk and Cultural Tradition." *Blackness and the Adventure of Western Culture.* Chicago: Third World Press, 1972.

Klotman, Phyllis R. "Langston Hughes's Jesse B. Semple and the Blues." *Phylon* 36 (1975): 68–72.

———. "Jesse B. Semple and the Narrative Art of Langston Hughes." *Journal of Narrative Technique* 3 (1973): 66–75.

Larkin, Margaret. "A Poet of the People—A Review." *Opportunity* 5 (March 1927): 84–85.

Locke, Alain. "The Weary Blues." *Palms* 4 (1926–27): 27–28.

Martin, Dellita. "Langston Hughes's Use of the Blues." *College Language Association Journal* 22 (1978–79): 151–59.

Miller, R. Baxter. "'Even after I was Dead': The Big Sea—Paradox, Preservation, and Holistic Time." *Black American Literature Forum* 11 (1977): 39–45.

———. " 'For a Moment, I Wondered': Theory and Symbolic Form in the Autobiographies of Langston Hughes." *The Langston Hughes Review* 3 (Fall 1984): 1–6.

———. *The Art and Imagination of Langston Hughes.* Lexington, Ky.: University Press of Kentucky, 1989.

Mullen, Edward J. *Langston Hughes in the Hispanic World and Haiti.* Hamden, Conn.: Archon, 1977.

Nichols, Charles H., ed. *Arna Bontemps and Langston Hughes: Letters 1925–1967.* New York: Dodd, Mead, 1980.

Nifong, David Michael. "Narrative Technique and Theory in The Ways of White Folks." *Black American Literature Forum* 15 (1981): 93–96.

———, ed. *Langston Hughes, Black Genius: A Critical Evaluation.* New York: William Morrow, 1971.

Peidra, Jose. "Through Blues." In *Do the Americas Have a Common Literature?* edited by Gustavo Perez Firmat. Durham, N.C.: Duke University Press, 1990.

Presley, James. "The Birth of Jesse B. Semple." *The Southern Review* 38 (1973): 219–25.

———. "Langston Hughes: A Personal Farewell." *Southwest Review* 54 (1969): 79–84.

Rampersad, Arnold. "The Origins of Poetry in Langston Hughes." *The Southern Review* 21 (Summer 1985): 695–705.

———. *The Life of Langston Hughes, 1902–1967.* 2 vols. New York: Oxford University Press, 1986–88.

Randall, Dudley. "The Black Aesthetic in the Thirties, Forties, and Fifties." In *The Black Aesthetic*, edited by Addison Gayle, Jr. Garden City, N.Y.: Doubleday (Anchor), 1972.

Redding, Saunders J. *To Make a Poet Black*. Chapel Hill: University of North Carolina Press, 1939.

Singh, Amritjit. "Beyond the Mountain: Langston Hughes on Race/Class and Art." *The Langston Hughes Review* 6 (Spring 1987): 37–43.

Smith, Raymond. "Langston Hughes: Evolution of the Poetic Persona." *Studies in the Literary Imagination* 7 (Spring 1974): 49–64.

Story, Ralph D. "Patronage and the Harlem Renaissance: You Get What You Pay For." *College Language Association Journal* 32 (March 1989): 284–95.

Tracy, Steven C. "Simple's Great Afro-American Joke." *College Language Association Journal* 27 (1983–84): 239–53.

———. "'Midnight Ruffles of Cat-Gut Lace': The Boogie Poems of Langston Hughes." *College Language Association Journal* 32 (Sept. 1988): 55–68.

Trotman, C. James, ed. *Langston Hughes: The Man, His Art, and His Continuing Influence*. New York: Garland Publishing, 1995.

Turner, Darwin T. "Langston Hughes as Playwright." *College Language Association Journal* 11 (1967–68): 297–309.

Wagner, Jean. "Langston Hughes." In *Black Poets of the United States from Paul Laurence Dunbar to Langston Hughes*. Urbana: University of Illinois Press, 1973.

Waldron, Edward E. "The Blues Poetry of Langston Hughes." *Negro American Literature Forum* 5 (1971): 140–49.

Walker, Alice. "Turning Into Love: Some Thoughts on Surviving and Meeting Langston Hughes." *Callaloo* 12 (Fall 1989): 663–66.

Winz, Cary D. "Langston Hughes: A Kansas Poet in the Harlem Renaissance." *Kansas Quarterly* 7 (Summer 1975): 58–71.

Index of
Themes and Ideas